"I Want to Kill Myself"

"I Want to Kill Myself"

*Helping Your Child
Cope with Depression
and Suicidal Thoughts*

TONIA K. SHAMOO

PHILIP G. PATROS

Lexington Books

D.C. Heath and Company • Lexington, Massachusetts • Toronto

Library of Congress Cataloging-in-Publication Data

Shamoo, Tonia K.
    "I want to kill myself" : helping your child cope with depression and
suicidal thoughts / Tonia K. Shamoo, Philip G.
Patros.
        p.   cm.
    ISBN 0-669-21130-3 (alk. paper)
    1. Teenagers—United States—Suicide behavior.   2. Children—
United States—Suicidal behavior.   3. Suicide—United States—
Prevention.   4. Depression in adolescence.   5. Depression in
children.   I. Patros, Philip G.   II. Title.
HV6546.S37   1990
362.2'87'083—dc20   89-29861
                                                                       CIP

Published simultaneously in Canada
Printed in the United States of America
Casebound International Standard Book Number: 0-669-21130-3
Library of Congress Catalog Card Number: 89-29861

The paper used in this publication meets the minimum requirements of
American National Standard for Information Sciences—Permanence of
Paper for Printed Library Materials, ANSI Z39.48–1984. ∞ ™

Year and number of this printing:

90 91 92 10 9 8 7 6 5 4 3 2

Dear Parents and Guardians,

In response to the interest expressed in our first book,
Depression and Suicide in Children and Adolescents
*(Allyn and Bacon), which was written for the school
systems, we have written this companion book for parents
and guardians.*
*We hope that this book will be of help to those who
need this type of information. Although all case studies
presented are composites of actual cases seen in our
practice (changed to ensure the confidentiality of the clients
and their families), they represent the types of problems
and behaviors presented by depressed and suicidal children
and adolescents.*

Contents

1

Do Kids Kill Themselves? Looking at Suicide

Suicide in Children

Depression. Suicide. Until recently parents never associated these words with their children, but today we're having an epidemic of depressed and suicidal young people. Why? What's happening to our youth? Do children really become depressed? Do they really commit suicide? As incredible as it may seem, they do.

Richie was a cute, red-haired, freckle-faced, five-year-old kindergarten student. His teacher became concerned when he began trying to cut himself with his scissors, and later stabbing himself with his pencil. When questioned about why he was trying to hurt himself, Richie explained that he wanted to go away, like his grandmother did. His mother was unhappy and said he was in the way. If he wasn't around, Richie reasoned, his mother could get married and be happy. Richie's mother did become involved in counseling, but the psychiatrist discounted Richie's suicide talk because "children that young don't kill themselves." Besides, what five-year-old child can plan or get the means to kill himself?

In the recent past, because information on depression and suicide for children one to twelve years of age was not available, it was widely disbelieved that children become depressed and can kill themselves. Medical and mental health professionals hold a number of false beliefs. Some of these beliefs are that (a) children below the age of ten don't kill themselves;[1] (b) that they don't have the strength or the means to plan a suicide;[2] (c) that the death concept is not formed and so they don't understand what death is or means; and (d) since their conscience is not fully developed, it is not possible for them to kill themselves. All these beliefs reflect the various theoretical views in the mental health profession.

> In the spring of his year in kindergarten, Richie had a plan and the means to kill himself. He rode his bike to school one morning fully intent on having an accident. Richie talked about his plan; he had it all figured out. As soon as school was over he planned to ride his bike to a particular street corner. The children had been cautioned several times about trucks speeding down the hill at that corner. Richie thought that he could wait at that corner until a big enough truck came down the hill and then he would ride his bike out in front of it. Richie's plan was to wait at the corner for a truck, his means was his bike.

Many professionals imply that children use suicidal behaviors to draw attention to their conflicts and that they are incapable of suicide. There are, in fact, more suicide attempts made by children than there are successes. More often children will make an attempt at suicide without meaning to complete it.[3] Children who use suicidal behaviors to call attention to their emotional pain may increase the intensity of their behaviors until that line between life and death is crossed.

> Richie was told that the adults in his life did not want him to die. His mother and her doctor were being called and he was not to leave the school building until arrangements were made for someone to drive him home. His teacher would wait with him. Unfortunately, Richie's teacher was distracted by another child and Richie left by the back door. Richie did ride his bike to that corner. Richie did wait for a big enough truck,

Richie did die. It was officially listed as a traffic accident. To spare those close to Richie, no mention of suicide was made.

Parents and authorities are surprised that children can and do kill themselves. Often they attempt to hide the cause of death if it is a suicide. This situation has partially influenced the collection of information for children's suicidal behavior. Present-day knowledge of suicide indicates that suicide is the tenth leading cause of death in children one to fourteen years old,[4] but it is felt that this statistic is an understatement of the true number of suicides. The underestimation of suicide rates in children may be related to the number of deaths reported as accidental; accidents are the leading cause of death among young children. In addition, various social, legal, and religious restraints may limit the accurate reporting of the causes of death.[5] For those children who threaten suicide, it has been estimated that there is an 8 to 10 percent increase in referrals to mental health clinics.[6,7] Also, about 12,000 children aged five to fourteen are admitted annually to psychiatric hospitals for suicidal behavior.[8] Again, these figures are believed to be an underestimation.

Children use a variety of ways to attempt and/or to commit suicide. They swallow various toxic materials, attempt to hang themselves, jump from heights, run into traffic, and cut or stab themselves. It has been documented that children over the age of nine are more likely to take medication or to ingest toxic or nontoxic material such as roach spray, rubbing alcohol, or even turtle food. Younger children are more likely to jump from buildings or run into traffic.[9,10,11,12]

Childhood is supposed to be a happy, carefree time, but as adults we may look back on our childhood and remember our own particular problems. The problems perhaps were similar to those faced by today's children: not being able to go to a friend's house, not having a date, feeling misunderstood. As parents, we planned that our children's childhood would be as happy as when we were growing up, or maybe happier. If we had an unhappy childhood, we would do things differently from our parents; we would be better.

Why, then, aren't our children happier? Why are they depressed? It comes as a surprise that our children aren't happy in spite of all that is done for them. Are we, the parents, the cause of our children's depression, or can the blame be placed on modern technology and life-styles?

Some authorities talk of four areas that they feel describe suicidal behaviors in young children:[13] (a) How attractive and enjoyable is the child's life? (b) Does the child experience mental and physical suffering? (c) Is the idea of death attractive, as viewed by the child's cultural and religious beliefs? (d) How afraid of death is the child?

Suicidal behavior in children is very complex. It is influenced by the interaction of the environment, the individual child's development, and the development of personality. Trying to separate out only one factor as a cause for depression and/or suicidal behaviors may be impossible. What is known is that if unsuccessful suicidal attempts are left unrecognized and untreated, the risk increases for other attempts and possible completions.[14] It is possible to change our intervention through better knowledge and understanding of depression in children.

Suicide in Adolescents

The depressed teenagers of today are probably the depressed children of last year. Depression is one of the most prevalent causes of adolescent suicide, as are the loss of parent and alienation from the family.[15] Depression in adolescents may stem from a wide range of situations that involve social interactions such as failure, guilt, loss of love object, or rejection. For some adolescents depression may be caused by biochemical imbalances.[16]

Alex was a hard-working, serious eighteen-year-old high school senior who had just received a scholarship to the college of his choice. Initially Alex was on top of the world, but later he became moody and withdrawn. Alex's boyhood friend had been killed a few months previously in a car accident, and on several occasions Alex had expressed guilt that he had not been with his friend. His parents felt that Alex seemed to have recovered from this experience and was devoting himself to his studies.

Often we, as parents, see only what we wish to see. It is difficult to recognize the depression that our teenager is feeling; it is even harder to see signals of suicide clearly. Such was the case of Alex and his parents. Fortunately, however, a successful intervention was made. Alex didn't understand himself and his feelings, but was able to ask for help. More important, his parents did not discount his feelings by making comments such as "Things will get better" or "Don't worry about it, give yourself some time." They didn't want to believe what they heard, but they did take action on Alex's feelings by getting professional help.

Thirteen-year-old Carol is repeating the seventh grade at her parents' insistence. Their major concern is her failing grades. The school's concern is her behavioral difficulties: for the past two years, Carol has received failing grades in all subjects, and her behavior has deteriorated.

Carol works hard at being the center of attention, both in school and at home. While in school she talks out loud in class, "smartmouths" the teachers, and refuses to do assignments.

Outside school, Carol has been involved in shoplifting and sexual activities. At home she is either in her room, with the stereo on at full volume, or on the phone. Her mother is concerned that Carol does not eat, but her father believes that she is not hungry because of all the junk food she eats during the day. Except for setting the table, Carol has no chores or responsibilities.

Is Carol a depressed teenager? She certainly doesn't fit the usual picture of depression. A person who is depressed should feel and look sad. Carol appears to be a rebellious, angry teenager, with "acting-out" behaviors. Such behaviors could be reflected in school problems, sexual promiscuity, substance abuse, running away from home, psychosomatic complaints, and difficulty with the law. Carol's behaviors were covering an underlying depression. Her emotional pain became too great for her to bear, and so suicide became her way of ending that pain.

In the past twenty years, the suicide rate for adolescents has increased drastically, whereas the overall suicide rate for the nation has remained fairly stable. More than one thousand teenagers a day attempt suicide; estimates indicate that eighteen of these attempts are successful. This figure translates to fifty-seven attempts every hour; approximately every hour and a half, one of our young people takes his or her life. There is some speculation that suicide attempts have risen as much as 3,000 percent a year.

Adolescents (aged thirteen to twenty-two) use a variety of methods to attempt suicide. Because it is frequently an impulsive act, they often use whatever means are available. It is generally felt that girls are less likely than boys to use a method that results in an immediate death. This point would explain why the rate of completed suicides is higher for adolescent boys than for girls (five to one): there is less time for intervention by others.[17] Most childrens' and adolescents' suicide attempts are made in the home, between 3:00 P.M. and midnight; this fact suggests that they hope to be saved.

The way in which females of all ages commit suicide has shown significant changes since 1980, but the males' methods have remained the same.[18] The leading method of suicide for males has consistently been firearms. In 1970, the leading method for females was poisoning, followed by firearms. In 1980 there was a reversal for females: the leading method became firearms, followed by poisoning. Some of the more commonly used methods are guns (40 percent), hanging (20 percent); drugs (17.5 percent), carbon monoxide (7.3 percent), jumping (7.2 percent), and drowning (2.4 percent). The peak times for youth suicide appear to be late fall and early winter, in contrast to the adults' peak time of spring. Almost a quarter of all youth suicides occur just before or after a birthday.[19]

Some adolescents have great difficulty in adjusting to the actual loss of a parent through death, divorce, or separation. Others have difficulty adjusting to the felt loss of a parent.

That is, even though the parent is still at home, he or she has withdrawn from them and/or the family psychologically, emotionally, or socially. With such a loss, some adolescents feel rejected; this feeling in turn leads to a sense of guilt and worthlessness. Loss of a parent removes the role model for many developing young people. The reasons for alienation from the family are many, and when family closeness and communication are undermined, suicide rates seem to rise.

Alcohol and drugs are closely related to suicide because they tend to reduce anxiety and psychological pain. There is a reduction of inhibitions, which allows the adolescent to express his or her anger and unhappiness more easily through suicidal behavior. Alcohol and drugs also allow suicidal impulses to be magnified, thus increasing the risk. The use of alcohol and drugs provides adolescents with a temporary, false security in dealing with their problems. Unfortunately, unless these individuals learn new and effective approaches, suicide may become an option.

Other factors, of course, affect adolescent suicide. Living in a highly mobile society prevents the establishing of stable roots. It is not uncommon for us, as practicing psychologists, to see children who have been in three to five different school systems in various parts of the world by the time they finish school. No sooner do they get adjusted and make friends than it's time to move. They are never in one place long enough to feel part of it. There are also difficulties in establishing an identity as to sex role. Years ago it was expected that boys placed certain games, acted in certain ways, and would do certain types of work when they grew up. The same expectations applied to girls. Today the games, the actions, and the work are mixed, so that children and adolescents are confused about how to act and function. Add to these the strong need to succeed and the fear of failing, the pressure to grow up too soon, and the stresses and demands imposed by family, friends, and school. This list is by no means complete, but it shows that the reasons for suicide are endless.

Experience has shown that individuals who attempt suicide give warning signs. Some signs are obvious; others even a trained professional would have trouble identifying. These warnings signs, which will be discussed later, are verbal, behavioral, and/or situational. Other behavior patterns are viewed as warnings that suicide may be contemplated.

Certification of Suicide

It is very difficult to collect statistics on suicide, especially for children. The reasons are many and varied. First, there is no standard criterion for determining whether or not a death was really a suicide. Often there is not enough information to determine the cause of a death. If a note indicating that the death was intentional is not left, the death may be viewed as a homicide, an accident, or of undetermined cause. Adolescent suicide notes are not common; in fact fewer than half of the adolescents who commit suicide leave a note.[20]

Another difficulty in determining whether a death is a suicide is that the family and/or the physician may be unwilling to give information to the medical examiner. The family may feel shame, confusion, guilt, and/or anger and may not want anyone to know.

In some instances, parents will deny that their child committed suicide. The denial is due to feelings of guilt; the guilt may be caused by assuming the responsibility of the suicide. The parents may feel that they weren't there for the child, that they should have done things differently, or that they should have recognized some of the warning signs. If they deny the suicide, they can protect themselves unconsciously from the guilt.

In addition, because there is a lack of clearly defined guidelines, two medical examiners using the same information may make different judgments as to whether or not a death is a suicide.

In some states the death is not ruled a suicide if a suicide note is not found. In another state, if a person is found hanged and if there are scratches around the neck and skin underneath the fingernails, the death is judged not to be a suicide. The reasoning behind this conclusion is that the person changed his or her mind and tried to stop the death.[21]

Social and cultural influences contribute to the confusion in determining whether a death is a suicide. Because of the taboo on suicide, many deaths are recorded as accidental in order to spare the family embarrassment, humiliation, and stigmatization. The stigma that is attached to suicide affects all social classes. Also, if a person dies hours, days, or even weeks after a suicide attempt, the cause of death might be officially listed, for example, as "death due to complications of surgery following gunshot wound to the head." For teens, death from auto accidents, substance abuse, or eating disorders are all possible suicides.

Suicide Clusters

Suicide clusters are groups of deaths that are closely related in time and space. To TV and newspaper journalists and others in the news media, a suicide cluster could include as few as two deaths. To others, a suicide cluster could be any series of three or more deaths.[22]

Suicide clusters are not new; probably the first recorded suicide cluster occurred around 1774.[23] Two hundred years later, one study found that there was a significant increase in the suicide rate after a suicide made front-page news, and suggested that publicity might influence or cause an increase in suicide rates.[24]

Another study examined the relationship between nationally televised news or feature stories about suicide and the fluctuation in the suicide rate among American teenagers before and after the broadcasts. It was found that the observed number of suicides by teenagers from zero to seven days after these televised broadcasts was significantly greater than expected.[25] The more networks carried the story, the greater the increase in suicides. Even so, there is no way of knowing whether the adolescents who took their lives had seen the broadcasts or whether the broadcasts prevented any suicides.

Another study of adolescent suicide clusters found that

most suicide clusters occurred in February.[26] For individual suicides, November is the peak month for persons age fifteen to twenty-nine, whereas May is the peak month for the general population.

Children and Adolescents at Risk

It is extremely difficult to identify children and adolescents who are at high risk for suicide. The study of suicide and suicidal behaviors in young people is relatively new, and there is very little literature in this area.

The following is known, however, about suicidal behaviors in children and adolescents:

1. The child may suffer the loss of a loved one or a significant person before he or she is twelve years old.
2. There is a poor communication pattern within the family.
3. The child has not learned how to handle problems.
4. The child may suffer greater physical, emotional, and psychological stresses than his or her friends, and does not know how to handle these stresses.

The following ten characteristics are common to adults who commit suicide.[27] We believe that they are also common to children and adolescents.

1. They suffer psychological or emotional pain that is so intense it seems as if it will never end.
2. Their needs for security, achievement, trust, and friendship are frustrated.
3. They see suicide rather than any other alternative as the solution for a problem.
4. They need to stop the pain they feel by ending their awareness or consciousness.
5. They feel helpless and hopeless in trying to deal with and stop the pain.

6. They see only two solutions to the problem: it is either solved or it is stopped by their death. This is black-and-white thinking.
7. They feel ambivalence. They want to live; yet they want to die.
8. They give clues about wanting to commit suicide.
9. They want to run away from the problems, fears, pain, and turmoil. Suicide is the ultimate runaway.
10. They have a lifelong pattern of coping poorly with problems.

Summary

Suicidal behavior is a distress signal. Children and adolescents are more likely to attempt to commit suicide, without really meaning to complete the act, than to succeed. The child or teen feels driven to perform a desperate act to call attention to problems that may have been overlooked or considered trivial by others. Signs almost always occur, but frequently they go unnoticed. Often the signals are given to several different people—a teacher, a friend, a parent—and so it is difficult to realize that suicide is being considered when a person gives only one signal. Signals are almost always given before a suicide attempt, however. They may be very specific, such as making a will or giving away possessions. Other signals may be less specific, such as changes in eating or sleeping habits, inability to concentrate, abrupt changes in personality, impulsiveness, slackening interest in schoolwork, decline in grades, absenteeism, loss or lack of friends, and (for older children) alcohol and drug abuse.

Suicidal behavior in children and adolescents is fast becoming America's number one mental health problem. Depression, once thought to be nonexistent in children, is now recognized as prevalent and appears to be an underlying factor in children's and adolescents' suicidal behavior and suicides.

Facts

- Children and adolescents attempt suicide more often than they succeed.
- There has been an 8 percent to 10 percent increase of children threatening suicide in referrals to mental health clinics.
- Suicide is the tenth leading cause of death in children one to fourteen years old.
- More than one thousand teenagers attempt suicide each day.
- Estimates indicate that eighteen of these adolescents' attempts succeed daily.
- Fifty-seven suicides are attempted every hour.
- Approximately every hour and a half, one of our young people takes his or her life.

2

Just a Bad Mood?
Looking at Depression

D EPRESSION is one of the leading causes of suicide. Some
mental health professionals believe, however, that children do not become depressed. It is only recently that the
American Psychiatric Association recognized depression in
children and adolescents as an illness. Even then, they used
signs of adult depression to diagnose it.

For some people, depression is just a bad or a down mood.
For others, it is a serious illness. It becomes serious when it
causes difficulty with work, friendships, family life, and/or
physical health. Major depression may last for a few weeks
or several years. Common symptoms may be great misery,
despair, and guilt. Depressed people feel totally worthless
and inadequate; they see little or no hope for the future and
they may have recurring thoughts about death and suicide.
Many of the people who commit suicide are suffering from
serious depression.

Depressed people may have frequent and perhaps even
irrational thoughts. For example, they may think that they
have lost all their money, are being punished for their sins,
or are dying of some incurable illness. Some depressed people do not admit to feeling any sadness or guilt, but they
withdraw from human contacts, lose all interest in life, and
can't seem to feel pleasure. Time passes slowly for them; the
world seems dreary and meaningless. Normal emotional responses, even grief, become impossible. They worry and are
irritable. They can't concentrate or make even simple decisions. They think about the same few ideas over and over

again. Their movements may be slow, with toneless speech and little, if any, facial expression. They may also be anxious and irritable; they may pace, moan, and wring their hands. Physical symptoms are common. Some depressed people are always tired, and can't eat or sleep. Others, however, overeat and oversleep. They may suffer from backaches, headaches, upset stomachs, or constipation. The symptoms vary with age. A recent article in the *Harvard Medical School Mental Health Letter* indicated that visits to doctors' offices by depressed people account for a large share of this country's medical costs.[1]

The American Psychiatric Association lists the following signs of major depression:[2]

1. A loss of interest or pleasure in the usual activities, as shown by being sad, blue, hopeless, or irritable.
2. Changes in appetite and/or weight patterns.
3. Altered sleeping patterns.
4. Increases in psychomotor agitation; behavior becomes fidgety and restless.
5. Loss of energy; listlessness or tiredness.
6. Self-reproach or excessive or inappropriate guilt. The child blames himself or herself for everything that goes wrong in his or her world.
7. Inability to concentrate; school performance may decline.
8. Recurrent thoughts of death or suicide.

Four of these signs must be seen nearly every day for at least two weeks. For children under age six, at least three of the first four should be seen. The reason for waiting two weeks is to make sure the signs are not normal, everyday behaviors. Also, separation anxiety may develop in school-age children and may cause the child to cling, to refuse to go to school, and to fear that he or she or the parents will die.

View One of Depression

One view of depression is that it does occur in childhood and that children's and adults' depressions are alike. It is suggested that there is actual sadness within the depressed child, just as within the depressed adult. This view also suggests that depressed children experience low self-esteem, irritability, weepiness, poor school performance, hopelessness, sleep and/or eating disturbances, fatigue, physical complaints, increased aggressiveness, and wetting and/or soiling of underclothes.

Although there is very little information about depression in early childhood, there is a growing realization that depression also exists in infancy and preschool children.

Tom is a nine-year-old fourth grader. His parents are divorced and he lives with his mother. Visits with his father are regular and consistent, and there is frequent contact between his parents concerning his schooling, discipline, and so on.

Tom recently had been dismissed from a learning disabilities resource room. His parents brought him to a psychologist because of behavioral difficulties, such as running away from home, destroying property, stealing from his mother, and getting into fights in school.

At the time the psychologist saw Tom, his behavior had changed. He had become more subdued and withdrawn from friends. He was not completing his schoolwork, and his grades began to reflect this. At home, Tom began to sleep on the floor either outside his mother's bedroom door or next to her bed. He missed his school bus in the mornings; upon returning home, he made frequent phone calls and demands to his mother at work. He began to whine and to make impossible requests of both his mother and his father. During this period his beloved cat died. Tom's stomachaches and headaches increased, and he was a frequent visitor to the school's health aide. He confided to the psychologist that he always felt sad and alone.

The end result of these behaviors occurred one evening when Tom's mother was busy preparing supper. Tom took a knife from the kitchen, destroyed a plant of his mother's, and then tried to cut himself on both wrists. Injuries were severe enough to warrant a visit to the hospital's emergency room.

View Two of Depression

A second view is that children cannot experience a long period of depression and that depression is a condition of childhood development that will disappear with time.[3,4] Children are seen as reacting to their environment; thus any depressive feelings and reactions are only temporary. Intellectual, emotional, and social development at different ages may make the signs of depression different in children than in adults.

It is difficult to determine whether depression in children and adolescents is temporary, how long it will last, or whether the depressed youth will grow up to be a depressed adult.

Michael is a kindergartner whose parents are separated. He lives with his mother and her boyfriend, Rich. There are frequent fights in the house; Rich, whom Michael adores, has left home several times, threatening never to come back. After a particularly bad argument, Rich left the house and became involved in a motorcycle accident that almost killed him. Michael was at the hospital with his mother and saw Rich immediately after the accident.

Soon after, Michael's behavior in school became disruptive and very agressive. He would explode in the classroom, throwing pencils and crayons and tearing papers. After the outburst he would crawl under the table or hide in the closet. Michael then began to run away from school. After the most recent incident he was found lying in a stream, wishing he were dead.

Masked Depression

The second view of depression also suggests that depression may not be expressed directly by children, but instead is "masked" and reflected in behaviors not associated with depression. Masked depression can be expressed as boredom, restlessness, fatigue, problems with concentration and behavior, and complaints of illness. From this point of view, many acting-out behaviors or conduct problems may be signs of depression. These problems may be shown in various ways, such as difficulty with authority, alcohol and/or drug abuse, sexual escapades, or truancy.

Chuck is a fourteen-year-old sophomore in high school who has become increasingly truant from school and is failing most of his subjects. He is disruptive both at home and in school. Explosive, angry outbursts include swearing, punching, and hitting his fist against the wall or door, and physical harassment of his parents. Chuck has become involved with alcohol and has had "a few beers," but denies any drug use.

According to his parents, Chuck was a "model child" before his sophomore year. He "toed the line," did his chores, studied, and generally kept himself out of trouble.

Chuck's father was a strict disciplinarian and allowed little deviation from his rules. His mother, although also strict, tended to treat Chuck like a much younger child, picking out his clothes, screening his phone calls, and searching his room weekly.

Chuck's developmental steps toward becoming independent and responsible were stymied. He received a message that he was not to be trusted and was not a responsible person. His attempts at talking to his parents only resulted in increasing his frustrations. No matter how hard he tried, he felt that he wasn't good enough and that the rules were always changing. If he cleaned his room, for example, he was promised that he could go out in that evening, only to find out that he had to stay in because he hadn't mowed the grass the previous Friday. Chuck's depression became so overwhelming that anger became a driving force.

Masked Depression or Learning Disability?

Some children who have a masked depression will develop learning and attention problems after having done well in school. These problems are like those found in children who

are labeled as having a specific learning disability or an
attention deficit disorder. They lose the ability to concentrate and pay attention, and they may suffer from hyperac-
tivity, distractibilty, and poor academic performance. An
important indicator is the age and grade level at which the
diagnosis is made. If records show average to good academic
performance in earlier years, this finding may suggest depression rather than any type of learning disorder.

Masked depression is a term sometimes used in cases of
drug abuse, alcoholism, delinquency, crime, and other disturbed or erratic behaviors when such behavior is thought to
hide depression or a mood disorder. A person who is suffering from a mood disorder views the world in such an extreme, pervasive, and sustained manner that his or her
reactions are affected.

Danny is an eleven-year-old sixth grade student who was referred to the school psychologist for academic difficulties. He
was described by his teacher as having a short attention span,
being highly distractible, and being unable to follow directions. Academic work in all areas, especially arithmetic, was
extremely poor. Peer difficulties were also noted.

Individual achievement testing showed that Danny was below grade level, whereas his intelligence tests displayed a
large discrepancy between his low-average performance IQ
and his superior verbal IQ. A classroom observation confirmed
the teacher's comments on Danny's high distractibility and
short attention span. Because of the school system's criteria
for psychoeducational testing and because of a large backlog
of referrals, no other testing was done, and no other information was collected. On the basis of this information, Danny
was placed in a learning disability resource room for one period a day.

Danny's behavior continued to deteriorate; soon he was at
the principal's office more often than in the classroom because
his disruptive behavior began to affect the other students. The
culmination occurred when Danny had a fight with the vice-
principal and ran away from school. He was missing overnight.

The school social worker made contact with the family. During this "informal" interview Danny's father revealed that

Danny's mother had left the house several months before and was living in another town with her boyfriend and "new son." Danny was deeply upset that he had been "replaced," but he felt loyal to his mother and could not talk of the desertion.

A review of Danny's prior academic achievements revealed that he had always been a B to C student. Group achievement tests also revealed that he was within grade level. Although on the surface Danny seemed to have a specific learning disability, depression was the main problem. Personality testing, information concerning prior behaviors and achievement, and a parental interview could have resulted in an appropriate placement.

Developmental Issues

As already mentioned, the American Psychiatric Association assumes that the essential features of depression are similar in infants, children, adolescents, and adults; there are, however, some differences.[5]

Depression in infancy is recognized by the child's sad appearance, immobility, and loss of appetite. The child also cries frequently and seems unable to be satisfied.

Although infancy depression is recognized clearly by facial expressions and behaviors, recognizing depression in children is much more difficult because of the many different symptoms. Some children may show acting-out behaviors; others may be seen as quiet, compliant, withdrawn, or shy. The common features of depression in both the acting-out and the quiet child seem to be mood disturbances and a lack of feeling or emotion. Many depressed children feel that they can't do anything right, and they are highly self-critical.

In adolescents, negative and antisocial behavior may appear. Feelings of wanting to leave home or of not being understood and approved of, restlessness, grouchiness, and aggressiveness are common. Sulking, being uncooperative with family, and withdrawal from social activities are likely. There may also be inattention to personal appearance and an increase in emotionality. Depressed adolescents may be very sensitive to rejection in love relationships. Abuse of alcohol or drugs may also develop.

Stress in Depression

Depression is often a reaction to a combination of many stress factors. One isolated incidence of stress does not mean that your child or adolescent will become depressed. If the child or adolescent is experiencing several stresses over a short period of time, however, such as a significant loss, family or personal conflicts, or a parent's physical or mental illness, the risk of depression could be high.

Confusion and conflict within the family due to social and economic problems can cause disruption and feelings of bewilderment and puzzlement. Adolescents as well as children are at a loss regarding what to expect and feel they receive little or no support.

Adolescents are concerned with their bodily image and have an idealized image of how they wish to look. Usually, adolescents are aware and concerned about the slightest physical change in complexion, weight or height, or breast or genital size.

Loss in Depression

For children and adolescents, the stress that can occur through loss is caused not only by the obvious loss of a significant person through death, divorce, separation, or family relocation, but also by a loss of childhood, loss of familiar boundaries and guidelines, loss of an ideal body image, loss of self-esteem, loss of goals, or even the loss of a pet.

The loss of childhood presents adolescents with physical, social, and emotional changes. The changes that go along with growth can be frightening to some individuals. New friendships and loyalties are formed outside the family. With the forming of these friendships comes a questioning of family standards and values. Adolescents feel the need to become more independent and to lessen their dependence on parents. With the increased independence comes increased responsibility; some adolescents may have very confused or ambivalent feelings. They feel a need to fit in with their friends and to find acceptance from them, along with balancing the stresses placed on them by parents, school, and society in general.

For both adolescents and children, a physical illness can cause a great deal of stress, especially if the illness sets them apart from their peers.

A loss of self-worth and self-esteem can be triggered by feelings of parental or peer rejection when expectations are not met. Just as adolescents are highly aware of the slightest physical change, they are also aware of their shortcomings and tend to exaggerate them. They often feel limited in what they are able to accomplish and are oversensitive to real or imagined criticism or rejection. Often parents reject a trait or a fault in their child or teenager that they sense within themselves. A woman may reject her daughter's femininity, perhaps because she is threatened or frightened by her own femininity. Parents may reject their child's ambitions because of their own felt inadequacies. Having a doctor in the family may be more important to the parents than the child's desire to be a teacher. Parents who do not listen to their child give the message that he or she is not worth listening to. Thus another blow to self-worth and self-esteem occurs.

Loss of goals can occur at any time, even when things are going well. This loss is hard to understand. When an adolescent achieves a goal, he or she should feel a sense of accomplishment. Instead, for some, there is a "so what?" feeling, accompanied by a sense of loss. Examples of letdowns are making the honor roll, finishing high school, or winning a dirt bike race. Sometimes victories are too stressful for vulnerable youths.

Physical Factors in Depression

There is general agreement that depression can show itself not only psychologically and behaviorally but physically as well. Because a strong tie exists between mind and body, emotional upsets can trigger a variety of physical illnesses.

These illnesses are real, and should not be dismissed lightly. Belittling or labeling a child or adolescent as a "baby" or a "hypochondriac" does not take away the pain.

Depression begins when the brain and body systems that govern mood and activity level are disturbed. Most people adjust when subjected to everyday stress; for these people, depression is a passing mood. If the stress is too much or if a person cannot adjust, the depression may grow deeper and may linger. The reason why some people become depressed while others do not may have a genetic basis. More to the point, however, there may be a combination of neurochemical imbalances, childhood losses, disappointments, and social conditions, which differs in degree in each case. Each of these factors constantly influences the others in ways that make it difficult to find the origin of the depression. Symptoms that look alike may have very different sources. For this reason many different kinds of treatment are helpful. Drugs and electrical shock therapy are used at the physical level; psychotherapy is used for thinking and relationships with other people.

Depression in children and adolescents does exist. According to recent estimates, from three to more than six million children and adolescents in the United States suffer from depression, most of which is unrecognized and untreated. Without intervention, how many of these young people will grow up to be depressed adults or to end their lives in suicide? Although not all depressed children and adolescents kill themselves, depression is still a major factor in suicide.

3

Death through a Child's Eyes

Children's Views and Attitudes toward Death

Young children who attempt or complete suicide do not really understand death. Most children under age five think of death as temporary and as lasting only a short time. Death is often seen as sleep, or simply as being less alive. Young children feel that people can move while in a coffin, even though the movement is limited. They also believe that dead people eat, breathe, and grow, and that they know what's happening on earth.

This type of thinking was seen in Beth, who was four years old at the time. While sitting in the family room and watching television, she suddenly burst into tears. When asked why she was crying, she said she had been thinking about dying and being dead. She wanted a promise that if she died, she would not be put in a "box." When asked why, her answer was that she wouldn't be able to breathe!

Young children do not understand the reality of death. Often they see it as a fantasy or as magical. They often think that after death they will be able to be invisible and to look down over any scene they wish. They believe they will be able to observe the effects of their death.[1] They also see death as an angel or as a dead person who still walks. In magical thinking a child wishes, for example, that somebody will die. Then if that person dies, the child feels that he or she made it happen by wishing. In a recent case, a depressed and suicidal fourteen-year-old girl with juvenile arthritis still showed magical thinking. When she was six years old and in the first grade, she had a recurring wish that she would get sick so she could stay home from school. Her arthritis was diagnosed in that year; the girl still believes that her wish caused her illness.

Most children feel some anxiety about death but are unable to talk about it, possibly because the anxiety and the fear are so great or because no one is willing to discuss it with them. Some children from the age of six to adolescence show their anxiety about death through a fear of bodily disfigurement and/or a loss of physical abilities and capacities.[2]

Even though children don't understand that death is permanent, the fact remains that they engage in suicidal behaviors for a variety of reasons including conscious and unconscious fantasies, wishes, and fears.

Suicide is often the end point of manipulation.[3] Children attempt to manipulate others in order to gain love and affection, to punish, or to change an impossible situation. They attempt manipulation in an effort to take control of a situation, especially one in which they feel helpless or believe that they are being taken advantage of.[4] "You'll be sorry when I'm dead" reflects the child's magical thinking; it expresses the fantasy of being in control and/or punishing others. The threat shows the child's limited understanding of the finality of death. It implies that he or she will survive or will be present to see the effects of the death on others.[5]

Adolescents' Views and Attitudes toward Death

Adolescents as well as children often see death glamorized by television, movies, books, and magazines. In many cases, adolescents romanticize death and the way it will affect loved ones and people in general. Often adolescents think of death as a peaceful sleep that will make everything better. They picture death as a way of punishing someone or as a way of forcing people important to them to express their love for them. Strangely, they believe that somehow they will be present to benefit from the punishment their death has caused or from the love that is shown.

It is not unusual for adolescents to gain great satisfaction from fantasies about death. Some children and adolescents see suicide and death as a way of being reunited with a parent, grandparent, sibling, girlfriend, or boyfriend who has died. They may also see it as a way of expressing their great love for someone who has died or who has rejected them. In early adolescence, some individuals think they will be present to witness the results of their suicide. Only a small percentage of adolescents age thirteen to sixteen seem to accept death as the complete end of life.

Many adolescents become preoccupied with thoughts of death and dying. They may even enjoy a sense of power over death in that they feel they can control when and where it will happen. By choosing, through suicide, when and where they will die, they achieve a sense of immortality. They also see death as an escape from their feelings of helplessness and hopelessness, so much so that they focus on it and then pursue it.[6]

Years ago most deaths took place in the home, where the dying person was surrounded by members of the family. Children and adolescents as well as adults were familiar with death; the experience helped them to view death as a normal part of living. In more recent years, most people have died in a hospital, and most children and adolescents reach adulthood without experiencing a death in the family. Many young people have never been present at someone's death, and that lack of experience makes it difficult to talk openly about death.

Most children and adolescents think of death as being far off. Most of their life is still ahead of them, and even though they understand that death is final, it's too distant to concern them. They are caught up in the everyday business of school, family, and social matters, enjoying the pleasures of the present. They are concerned more with the quality of life than with how long they will live. At this age they are attempting to become independent of their family and to plan for the future. They don't have time to focus on death unless it happens to someone they can identify with. Even then, they see it as only a short-term process. It isn't unusual for adolescents to be caught up emotionally in the death of a fellow student who is killed in an automobile accident and then to speed dangerously down the highway the day after the funeral. Adolescents also continue using and abusing alcohol and drugs even if a friend or an acquaintance died from substance abuse. They deny death through a feeling of immortality, even though they are aware of the reality of death.

Adolescents see death as something that happens to others; their great concern with the present makes the future and the past relatively unimportant. Although adolescents are aware that death is a final process for all living things, they, like most other people, repress that knowledge and go about their lives. Generally many years must pass after adolescence before the reality and the acceptance of death become part of one's concept of life. This reality is repressed as long as possible.

Seeing the adolescents' concept of death in this manner, one can understand that unusual pressure and stress would be needed to make them think of death in present-day terms. Such thinking would disrupt a normal growth process and would make them face their own mortality and fear of death.

Death as a Choice

Children and adolescents use death as an escape from an intolerable living situation. Young people who show suicidal behavior have fewer inner resources during stressful times; they have difficulty in coping and in communicating their discomforts or problems.[7] In early adolescence and possibly even earlier, there is an intensity in all feelings, such as anger, sadness, and helplessness. Children and adolescents see death as the only way out because they have so few life experiences and such poor problem-solving techniques.

Timmy is a nine-year-old boy with an alcoholic mother who provides only sporadic care. His father disappeared from the family before Timmy's birth.

Blamed for events that had gone wrong in his mother's life, Timmy became the focus of her anger. Physical abuse was a way of life. In an attempt to escape from his mother, he began to stay out on the streets.

While on the streets, Timmy quickly became a target for street gangs. Both his home and the street were dangerous places. The only life he experienced was beatings by his mother and the dangers of the street.

Timmy was admitted to the hospital's emergency room because of drug overdose. When questioned, he expressed the wish to die. The future, as Timmy perceived it, was bleak, with no hope and no help.

Death as Related to Loss

The misunderstanding of death may cause any type of loss to be reason for suicide. It need not be the loss of a parent; it could be that of a friend, of a pet, or even of status or self-esteem.

To children, loss of status or self-respect because of a low grade in school can be just as real as a death. Loss also can occur when they feel that they have been let down by someone on whom they depend.[8] Because children feel rejection so strongly, even this can be seen as a serious loss. Rejection can come from anywhere—friends, family, or acquaintances. It can even come from someone the child or adolescent doesn't know but would like to know. Whatever the loss, the result is a strong feeling of hopelessness, and death may be seen as the only solution.

Anna, a senior in high school, was an A student. Her parents did not allow her to be involved in any extracurricular activities; she was under constant pressure for high academic achievement. Her parents insisted on grades no lower than an A− average. Homework took priority over all nonschool activities.

Anna was having difficulty in a geometry course, but could not bring herself to ask for help because she felt that she should be able to handle it by herself. She failed the midterm examination and consequently received a C on her report card. Her parents insisted that she limit social activities and concentrate on pulling up her grade. Anna was made to feel that she had not applied herself, although she believed she had put in a great deal of effort. In addition, she broke up with her boyfriend and was rejected by one of the colleges she had selected. Feeling a loss of status and self-respect, and seeing no relief from parental pressure, Anna attempted suicide.

Role Reversal

Some families have difficulty with parenting. The roles seem to be reversed: the parents look for emotional support, guidance, and approval from their children. The parents are so emotionally needy that they allow the children to assume the parental role. This is found to be a common occurrence in families where children exhibit suicidal behaviors.[9]

Melissa, twelve years old and in the sixth grade, was always described by her mother as "bossy." Melissa was referred to a mental health clinic after she had attempted to hang herself.

In the initial interview it became apparent that Melissa had taken on the responsibility of parenting her mother. She explained that her mother "couldn't hold it together" and that she was tired of always listening to her mother talk about "the day's problems and hassles, bills, her father, how unhappy she is, and why she can't get any dates." Melissa would come home from school, clean the house, baby-sit her baby brother, and start dinner. At night she would "permit" her mother to go out, staying alone and supervising the younger child.

Melissa never had time for herself or anyone to confide in. She was seldom called, had few friends, and had very little in the way of social activities.

Melissa became overwhelmed, not only with the responsibilities of adulthood, but also with being her mother's mother.

4

Myths and Misinformation about Suicide

T HERE are many commonly accepted myths about suicide and much misinformation. One way to deal with the problem of suicide is by correcting the myths and misinformation and by removing the mystery.

The following list of myths is not intended to be complete, but will deal with some of the more widely accepted beliefs. We hope that bringing to light such myths will result in more knowledge and greater acceptance of the seriousness of childhood and adolescent suicide.

Myth: People Who Talk about Suicide Don't Do It

It's difficult to believe that your child or adolescent means to kill him- or herself. How would you know that your son or daughter intends to commit suicide when they make such common statements as "I'll kill myself if John doesn't call me tonight" or "I wish I were dead"? Usually it's difficult to know; that's why it's so important to ask. It's always better to risk asking a "dumb" question than to have your child attempt suicide. Signals are usually sent; the hope is that these signals will be heard and listened to. Any suicide threat must be taken seriously. When young people's words fail to get the message across that they are hurting, they may attempt suicide. Studies of completed suicides among children and adolescents show that most of them had talked about their wish to die or had even threatened suicide.[1]

Consider Bobby, who kept telling his mother that he wished he was dead. He made this statement a number of times, but he always laughed and said he was joking. The laughter and the jokes convinced his mother that he was only fooling; unfortunately she did not stop to ask Bobby if something was really bothering him. It did not occur to her to look for any help. Bobby did make an attempt on his life.

Any statements about dying made repeatedly over a period of time, especially if your child's mood or behavior pattern has changed, should be followed up with concerned questions and possibly with outside professional help. *Remember: People who talk about suicide do kill themselves.*

Myth: Suicidal People Are Fully Intent on Dying

Children and adolescents who are depressed and/or suicidal have mixed feelings about dying. They want to live, but living is too painful. They want to die, but they are afraid to do so. Most suicides occur in the home and at a time when help might be possible. Often the youth calls for help immediately after a suicide attempt. This reaching out is a way of showing confusion about living or dying. Young people often look at the pros and cons of living before deciding on suicide, but even then they are not sure that suicide is the answer.

Often children call a suicide hotline for help after ingesting pills. John did just that after taking a full bottle of over-the-counter pain relievers. Still having mixed feelings about suicide, he refused at first to identify himself or to give his address. Only after some intervention by the hotline volunteer did he give the information necessary to send help. *Remember: People with suicidal thoughts don't really want to die.*

Myth: People Need Only to Look on the Bright Side of Life to Feel Better

This is a very simplistic view; such a comment, when made to a suicidal child or adolescent, says that no one knows how he or she really feels. Children and adolescents do not have enough life experience to realize that situations and feelings change. Being told that "things will look better tomorrow" only causes the depressed youth to feel more isolated and more alone with his or her feelings. No one understands the pain that is felt because no one listens to what is being said. This is hearing without listening.

Jim, an adolescent, was depressed and told his teacher that he had thought of suicide. The teacher responded by pointing out all of his good qualities and mentioning the many things that he should be thankful for. He also said, "You're in a slump and things will get better." The teacher pointed out that Jim's senior year was coming up and then college, and said that because of Jim's excellent sports record he might be able to win a scholarship.

This approach doesn't take into account that Jim was thinking of the present, not of the future. College was too far away. Many children and adolescents do not think of the future; they want or can deal only with the present. Looking on the bright side is not always possible because their problems and emotions are crippling. These youths are simply unable to see or think of the bright side. This approach may make them feel even more depressed and guilty because it is suggested that they should not feel as they do. *Remember: A depressed and suicidal person may be able to think about the good things of life but not to believe in them.*

Myth: People Who Make Suicide Attempts Are Only Looking for Attention

Unfortunately, many adults believe that children's and adolescents' suicides are accidents and that the youths did not really mean to hurt themselves. It is thought that these individuals were fooling around and merely wanted attention. Everyone wants attention, but for children and adolescents who feel ignored, hopeless, desperate, and isolated, suicide becomes a real choice. It is not only deadly but sad if the only way our children can get attention is to fool around with self-destructive behaviors. A suicide attempt suggests that other ways of getting help have been tried and have failed. The young person sees no other alternative but suicide as a way of easing his or her intense pain. It seems that children's and adolescents' ability to handle pain is extremely low, possibly because physical pain is often eased quickly by medication. When they find no medication to take away the emotional pain or when they find that no one is willing or able to help them, they may attempt suicide. While a successful suicide ends the pain, a suicide attempt is a cry for help. This cry needs to be listened to and answered.

Consider the diabetic girl who found that she was pregnant and that her boyfriend wanted nothing to do with her. She took an overdose of insulin and was rushed to the emergency room. She said that she took double the prescribed amount because she thought she had forgotten her morning dose. The staff at the emergency room felt that she was depressed and that the overdose was an attempt at suicide. She admitted to the emergency room staff that this was so, but denied it when her parents arrived. The parents believed that their daughter was simply upset because of the pregnancy and wanted to get her boyfriend's attention. Against the hospital staff's advice and recommendations, the parents did not seek further help. *Remember: Children and adolescents who attempt suicide are usually in intense emotional pain and are not merely looking for attention.*

Myth: When the Depressed Person Begins to Show Signs of Improvement, the Crisis is Over

In this case, a person who is depressed seems to be improving. Behavior problems may lessen, or the individual will be seen as beginning to deal with his or her drug or alcohol problem. In fact, however, many suicides occur within a few months of this improvement. The reason for the improvement may simply be that the suicidal person has decided to complete the suicide. Such a person feels great anxiety while attempting to make a decision.

Once the decision is made, regardless of what it is, the individual feels less anxiety. This is what happens to suicidal persons when they seem to be improving. This period of improvement is a very dangerous time because it may suggest that a decision to commit suicide has been made. Also, once a person feels less depressed, he or she may have more energy to carry out a suicide plan; thus the risk may be greater.

A concerned parent made an appointment to talk about her daughter, who seemed to be depressed. At the first visit the mother said that in the past few days things had been much better, and maybe she had overreacted. Her daughter was no longer depressed, and things were going better at home and at school. Because the time when the depression seems to be lifting is important for any person who may be suicidal, the daughter was interviewed. She admitted that she had decided to commit suicide. *Remember: Suicide is still a possibility, even though a person seems to be feeling or acting better after a period of depression.*

Myth: Talking about Suicide Puts the Thought into People's Heads

Many people think that talking about suicide will increase the possibility of its happening. They are afraid that talking about it with a child or a teenager will put the idea into their minds. If young people are giving clues by their behavior that they are thinking about suicide, it would seem that the idea is already there. It's very likely that their behavior is a way of getting adults to talk to them about their feelings and fears. If an adult doesn't do so, they receive the message that no one really cares.

An example is Debbie. She was becoming more and more withdrawn and anxious, and her mother asked her about this new behavior. When asked whether she was thinking about hurting herself, Debbie admitted that she was, but felt relieved that her mother knew and was not afraid to talk with her.

Another example is Mike, who showed some of the same behavior as Debbie. When he was asked about this behavior, he was surprised by his mother's concern. He was simply feeling a lot of stress from school and a new part-time job. When his mother asked about suicide, Mike said that he felt too good about himself to do anything so stupid but he appreciated his mother's concern.

Even though Mike was not suicidal, it was better for his mother to trust her feelings and ask than to have her suspicions proved true by an attempted suicide. *Remember: Talking about suicide with children and adolescents will not put the idea into their heads.*

Myth: Children Don't Know How to Kill Themselves, nor Are They Strong Enough

Most adults believe that children don't know how to kill themselves. They also believe that many young people do not understand that death is final. Thus, they reason, any attempt that children and adolescents make on their life is not real, nor do they mean to complete it.

There is enough evidence at present to show that this is not true. If children have suicidal ideas, they will admit it. This finding suggests that they know enough to kill themselves. We recommend that parents begin to question their children concerning "accidents"; many deaths that have been called accidental may have been suicides. In our private practice we have seen children who gave evidence of thinking, planning, and carrying out a suicide attempt. Parents need to be aware enough to ask important questions.

A case mentioned in chapter 1 is an example of a child with the capacity to kill himself. Richie and his mother were referred to a mental health clinic by a school psychologist. Richie told the school psychologist a number of times that he was going to ride his bike in front of a truck so he could kill himself and make his mother "happy." He finally succeeded in taking his life, just as he said he would. *Remem-*

ber: Children and adolescents do know how to kill themselves.

Myth: People Who Attempt Suicide Are Mentally Ill

Children and adolescents who attempt suicide are often thought of as socially or emotionally maladjusted. They often rebel against seeking professional help because they are afraid they will be seen as having serious emotional problems. Other than being socially or emotionally disturbed, there are many reasons why children attempt suicide. Stress, loss of a loved one, or any failure are examples. Only a small percentage of adults who attempt and complete suicide have serious psychological problems. There is no evidence to date that this is not also true for children and adolescents.

Dennis is a boy of high school age whose parents are in the process of a divorce. He recently broke up with his girlfriend, lost his part-time job, did not make the varsity basketball team, and was failing in some of his classes. Although Dennis was usually seen as a happy-go-lucky boy, the stress he was suffering caused him to be depressed and to contemplate suicide; nothing was going right. It was the stresses—not mental illness—that caused him to consider taking his own life. *Remember: Most children and adolescents who attempt to kill themselves do so because of stress, not mental illness.*

Myth: When a Child Develops Any Serious Acting-out Behaviors or Emotional Problems or Attempts Suicide, the Parents Are Responsible

Many parents hold themselves responsible for their children's actions; they ask themselves where they went wrong. Many people also hold parents responsible for their children's behavior. This view adds to parents' guilt and feelings of responsibility. As we have long known, parents are often the last to see any danger signs in behaviors that may cause pain or problems for their children. We have never seen any parents who deliberately set out to cause difficulty for their children. Parents use their best judgment in deciding what is right at the time. They are not at fault if things do not turn out favorably.

In our work with survivors of children who kill themselves, we often see parents who keep replaying the circumstances of their child's suicide and their responsibility for it. They blame themselves and keep thinking about the details that may or may not have made a difference. By doing so, they stop the pain from healing. At this stage we must convince parents that they did their best.

Recently we saw a woman who felt she had to be both mother and father to her children since her divorce. When her son made an attempt on his own life, she was overwhelmed by her sense of guilt. She believed she had failed to fill the gap left by her ex-husband and to meet all her son's needs. In addition to taking care of the house and raising the children, she held a full-time job. She could not see the reality of the situation; she felt that she had to be all things to all people, the "super mom" (and dad). *Remember: Parents cannot be responsible for all the behaviors of their children.*

Myth: Substance Abuse or Aggressive and Hostile Behaviors Are Outlets for Anger and Thus Reduce the Possibility of Suicide

Many children and adolescents use drugs or alcohol to ease their pain and to escape from dealing with life in general. Because alcohol and many drugs are depressants, they make a depressed person even more depressed and increase the risk of suicide. Angry, aggressive behavior is a way of saying that a youth is hurting as well as a way of seeking immediate attention. These behaviors are usually a way of showing that the young person is unable to deal with the stresses in his or her life. Drug or alcohol abuse is also considered a form of slow or hidden suicide. In addition, it gives young people a false sense of courage; it removes inhibitions and makes them less fearful of death.

Scott was an angry young man who frequently acted out and alienated everyone around him. He disrupted classes, rebelled against family and school, and was in trouble with the law for the use of drugs and alcohol. This behavior did not satisfy his anger and frustrations but made him even more isolated because many of his peers wanted nothing to do with him. Scott did not see his behavior as responsible for the alienation he suffered; he blamed others and became more involved with drugs and alcohol. Feeling unable to adjust to his environment, he felt that the only solution was suicide. *Remember: Drugs and alcohol increase the possibility of an attempt in a suicide-prone youngster.*

Myth: Childhood and Adolescence Are a Carefree, Trouble-free Time of Life, Filled with Only Minor Problems and Adjustments

Adults often fail to see the fears and anxieties faced by children and adolescents as they attempt to adjust to a more complex and confusing world. More advanced technology, more violence, higher educational demands, more readily available and greater use of drugs and alcohol, greater threats of venereal disease, increased peer pressure, the climbing divorce rate, and more family disruptions are only a few of the things affecting today's children and adolescents.

Not all children come from happy homes. Nine-year-old Sue lives with her mother and her mother's boyfriend. She doesn't see her father very often, and her relationship with her mother is poor because of her mother's boyfriend and his abuse. Sue is often left alone; she is not adequately clothed or fed, and her personal hygiene is poor. She is picked on at school, and her teachers make impossible demands; often she soils herself. This causes her embarrassment and results in teasing by other students. She spends afternoons and evenings in a home that is neither clean nor happy. This is hardly a carefree time for a child. *Remember: Many children and adolescents are unhappy and have adjustment problems.*

Myth: Once People Contemplate or Attempt Suicide, They Must Be Considered Suicidal for the Rest of Their Lives

The fact is that most people, children and adolescents included, think of suicide for only a limited time. Once the crisis has passed and the reasons for considering suicide are resolved, their suicidal thinking usually stops. Although this may generally be true, we believe that once suicide becomes a strong option for dealing with one's problems, it will remain an option but will have less priority. Future problems will be handled in a number of ways; when these fail, suicide again may be an option.

We believe that many people, including children and adolescents, deal with problems according to some kind of priority. Methods that have been highly successful in the past will continue to be used. If for some reason these methods fail, suicide may become a priority option. When individuals are thinking about suicide, it ranks high as a way of dealing with problems. Once they have resolved the problem that caused them to consider suicide and have replaced ending their lives with better ways of dealing with stresses, suicide is no longer a high-priority option. Therefore, although suicide is moved to a much lower position in their ranking of problem-solving techniques, we believe that for some individuals it never completely disappears as an option.

Adults often come to us for therapy after an attempted suicide. When we questioned them, we usually find that this is not their first attempt. Many have attempted suicide in the past, even years before the latest incident. *Remember: Suicide may continue to be a way of dealing with problems even after the crisis is over.*

Myths and Facts about Suicide

Myth	*Fact*
People who talk about suicide don't do it.	People who *do* talk about suicide *do* kill themselves. Talk of suicide, of not wanting to go on anymore, of despair, and of hopelessness are cries for help. These are signals that need to be taken seriously.
Suicidal people are fully intent on dying.	There is an ambivalence about dying. People need to end the pain, but there is always the wish that something or someone will remove the pain so that life can continue.
People only need to look on the bright side of life to feel better.	For those who are thinking of suicide, it is difficult, if not impossible, to see the bright side of life. To acknowledge that there is a bright side confirms and conveys the message that they have failed; otherwise their life, too, could have a bright side.
People who make suicide attempts are only looking for attention.	It is true that such people are looking for some attention, but they are also looking for a way to ease the pain, for someone to hear their cries for help.

When the depressed person begins to show signs of improvement, the crisis is over.

When a person's mood or behavior "picks up," it may be because the indecision concerning suicide is over. A decision has been made and the anxiety is past. That decision could be *for* suicide.

Talking about suicide puts the thought into people's heads.

If the clues are being broadcasted, talking about suicide won't put the thought there. It is there already. Talking about suicide removes people's fears that they are crazy and alone, and also takes away the guilt for thinking that way.

Children don't know how to kill themselves.

Children do know how to hurt and/or kill themselves. Television provides the model, means, and methods. Significant others in a child's life may also provide the model of suicide as a way of solving a problem.

People who attempt suicide are mentally ill.

People who attempt suicide are stressed beyond their coping abilities. They aren't necessarily mentally ill. Depressed, yes; stressed, yes; but rarely mentally ill.

Parents are responsible if their child attempts suicide.

Parents do the best they can with the information

and coping skills they have. There is often denial and disbelief because the thought of suicide is so frightening. Also, some parents are too fragile emotionally and psychologically to meet their children's needs.

Substance abuse and/or acting-out behaviors are outlets for anger and thus reduce the possibility of suicide.

These behaviors are signs of poor adjustment and reflect the frustrations these people feel. When the drug/alcohol abuse and/or acting-out behaviors are unsuccessful for dealing with their hurt and problems, suicide becomes a greater possibility.

Childhood and adolescence are a carefree, trouble-free time of life, filled with only minor problems and adjustments.

Children are no longer protected as much from outside influences as they once were. They are exposed to the harsh realities of the world at ages when they are most impressionable; thus their fears and anxieties are increased.

Once people contemplate or attempt suicide, they must be considered suicidal for the rest of their lives.

When the crisis is over and the problems leading to suicidal thought are resolved, suicidal ideation usually ceases. It is possible, however, that suicide still will be a subdued option for an individual, but as long as coping skills are adequate, it is not acted on. When coping skills fail, suicide again may become a strong option.

5

Is My Child Depressed?

DEPRESSION happens to people of all ages, even infants. In a case we were involved in recently, a baby was abandoned by her mother at birth. The father took the baby and gave it to his sister, who had no children, to raise. The father later disappeared. After a year, the natural mother decided that she wanted her baby back, and after several months of legal involvement gained custody of the baby. When the baby was returned to the mother, she was fourteen months old. Several months later the baby was admitted to a local hospital for "failure to thrive." She had stopped eating and had to be tube-fed. The baby is now almost two years old and is still not eating. She is a beautiful little girl, who only speaks in a very depressed monotone voice. She has no interest in playing with toys, and does not respond to people. Is she depressed? We feel that she is.

Depression, in general, is not an occasional feeling of being down or blue. It is a serious illness and often a factor in suicide. Depression affects children and adolescents as well as adults. The following signs are not intended to be all-inclusive but are typical indications of child and adolescent depression. Consideration of the seriousness of any behavior must include the child's or adolescent's age, family environment, social environment, the length of time the behavior has been seen, and the youth's general emotional adjustment.

Although many of the behaviors listed here are generally normal in young people, they become significant when they show up in extremes or as a change from what is usually seen.

Signals of Depression

Lack of Interest. The usual pleasant activities are no longer enjoyable for depressed children or adolescents. They lose interest in almost everything, at home, in school, and socially. It is almost impossible to motivate them. They complain a lot and are easily bored. They change from being generally cooperative to not wanting to do anything or to be involved with the family or with anything the family does. In general, depressed youths lack enthusiasm for just about anything. There is often a change in attitude toward school and academics.

Possible Home Indicators. Your child or adolescent appears to be daydreaming or "cut off" from family discussions and activities. Chores are forgotten and are not done. If they are done, they are done poorly and/or it takes a long time to complete them. Although spending a lot of time alone in their bedroom is common for adolescents, it is unusual in young children. Spending a great deal of time alone, without family or friends, is not appropriate for either child or adolescent. Slowness in physical movements may also be seen. The child may be listless, with an increase in disruptive behavior. He or she may become easily distracted; attention and concentration may be poor. More than usual, the child may not hear what you're saying, may miss explanations or directions, or may even distort what has been said.

Change in Appetite. Children or adolescents will pick at their food and eat very little, complaining that they are not hungry. Foods that they usually enjoy are no longer appealing. At the other extreme, they will not only eat meals but look around for more food. Even though they are not hungry, they will eat whatever is available or will continually want something to eat.

Possible Home Indicators. A change in appetite is evidenced in your child's or adolescent's increased appetite and concern about food or by a lack of appetite and disinterest in food. The important thing is the change from usual food habits. These youths might eat their own lunch and help others finish theirs. At school, they may steal lunches or snacks or borrow money from friends to buy additional lunches or snacks. At home, they may hide food in their rooms—under the bed, in the closet, or in the bureau. Overall, they seem to have a constant but vague need to eat.

At the other extreme, your child or adolescent might begin to give away lunches at school or avoid eating at home. He or she will give various reasons for not eating, such as "not hungry," "have a stomachache," or "already full." The child or adolescent might listlessly push around food on a plate, or tear a sandwich or bread into little pieces and roll them into little balls. Some youths deliberately spoil food.

Change in Sleep Pattern. This change may take the form of restless sleep, not being able to fall asleep at night, and/or waking up in the early morning hours and being unable to go back to sleep. These children and adolescents have little energy and always seem tired. Excessive sleep may be another symptom. The child or adolescent may appear to be pale and to have a low activity level with little motivation or interest, even in things that were formerly fun.

Possible Home Indicators. Your child or adolescent might fall asleep during any type of passive activity, such as watching TV, reading, or listening to music. These young people yawn frequently and display listless, restless behavior; their energy level is low. They show a lack of interest and/or involvement in family affairs. Often they avoid their chores and/or responsibilities. Perhaps they miss school or are late because of oversleeping. Even when they go to school, they may fall asleep in class and/or seldom do much classwork. They lag behind everyone else; poor attention and concentration may be noted.

Loss of Energy. Some children and adolescents who are normally active and alert will show an apparent listlessness and tiredness. They may verbalize this loss of energy by complaining that they are too tired, are not interested, or are bored. In many cases, they do not express this feeling verbally but simply behave in a way that shows a low energy level.

Possible Home Indicators. Tired and/or restless behavior is evidenced in chores or responsibilities that are not carried out or are done poorly and too quickly. Your child or adolescent may be sleepy or may fall asleep at odd times during the day. Because of the lack of energy, he or she may put off tasks until the next day and may become disorganized as things begin to pile up. Even when given extra time to complete a task, these youths are unable to maintain an appropriate energy level. Often they are the last ones to do anything, such as dressing, showering, or cleaning their room. Again, they show poor attention and concentration.

Blaming Oneself Inappropriately. The child or adolescent takes the blame for everything that goes wrong, not only in his or her life but in everyone else's. Such youths are very critical of themselves and of their behavior; the result is a low opinion of themselves.

Possible Home Indicators. Your child or adolescent may show withdrawn or sullen behavior. He or she may become defensive or passive. The child may be highly self-critical and may believe that he or she is different from others of the same age. These youths appear to have the weight of the world on their shoulders. They are quick to react to any kind of pressure with tears, and they become easy targets for other children because they lack confidence in themselves. They become extremely sensitive and worry about everything; they may appear touchy and fretful, and are easily upset by surprises or by any changes in a routine. Often these children believe that they are not accepted by anyone and take any criticism personally, as though there was something wrong with them. They can't be reasoned with; often they hold onto a hurt, nurse a grudge, or talk or mutter under their breath.

Negative Feelings about Self. Negative feelings in children and adolescents are shown in feelings of worthlessness. These young people feel as though they are unloved and unwanted by everyone. Their relationships with others tend to be poor because they often feel used. They withdraw socially because they feel uncomfortable in most relationships, and they have trouble maintaining long-term relationships. These youths feel strongly that they are not liked or accepted.

Possible Home Indicators. These children do not stand up for themselves and are usually afraid to say "no" to friends. Their peer relationships are poor; they may be uncomfortable even with brothers and sisters. They cover up their feelings of worthlessness by being very defensive. They may also be very critical of others, especially siblings, and are quick to point out mistakes or misbehaviors. They become intolerant, even (at times) of their parents. Such youths feel that their siblings are favored over them and that their parents give more to the siblings than to them. It is not unusual to see angry outbursts at any hint of rejection, real or imagined.

Feelings of Sadness, Hopelessness, and Worry. Children and adolescents with these feelings look and feel unhappy. They feel rejection and helplessness in dealing with life circumstances. They appear withdrawn and inhibited as well as fearful. These young people worry not only about themselves but also about things over which they have little control.

Possible Home Indicators. Your child or adolescent may look and feel sad and unhappy. He or she will give up easily and will need encouragement to attempt and complete any task. Children with these feelings may be disorganized because of the inability to concentrate or pay attention to what's going on. When mistakes are pointed out or when a job is not done right, they tend to feel overwhelmed when asked to do it over. They feel that they can't do anything right and believe that they will not be accepted by others.

Often they feel unable to do something they had previously done successfully. They feel defeated or unsuccessful even before getting started. Your child or adolescent may feel disturbed by everything, not only by a specific issue. There are poor peer relationships and sibling difficulties; these children or adolescents act frightened. They have a constant need for emotional support from a parent or parents.

Inability to Concentrate or Pay Attention. Poor ability to pay attention is often reflected in not remembering directions or instructions. These children frequently forget to do things they are asked to do, even within a short time. There may even be a drop in school grades because they have difficulty focusing on schoolwork. In fact, they have difficulty focusing on almost anything because their thoughts are affected by their fears and concerns.

Possible Home Indicators. Your child or adolescent may take a long time to complete any chore because he or she is easily distracted. Often these young people forget things or lose things. They may start one activity or job only to stop it and start another, and never finish anything. They often seem to be scattered in their thinking; responsibilities are often forgotten. Such children have trouble following directions and may not appear to be listening. Left to themselves, they have difficulty carrying out jobs, responsibilities, and/ or instructions. They can't be relied upon to work independently. Often they misinterpret comments and/or instructions, arguing or saying, "You didn't say that." Because of disorganization and anxiety, these children may seem to be constantly in motion, and may be seen as hyperactive by the parent and/or the school system. Their restless behavior is agitated and disorganized.

Morbid Thoughts. Beyond normal curiosity, children and adolescents are normally not concerned with death. Depressed youngsters often have thoughts of death and/or suicide, however, and dwell on these thoughts excessively.

Possible Home Indicators. Your child or adolescent may be fearful and may overreact to someone's death. He or she may talk or write about morbid death themes, or they may be evident in drawings and pictures. Some children may draw dismembered bodies or gruesome scenes. They may show great interest or excitement about terrorists or war actions. On more than one occasion and within a short time, they may focus on death, dying, suicide, or the worthlessness of life through music, reading, movies, or television. Adolescents in particular may isolate themselves in their rooms, playing music with morbid overtones over and over again.

Masked Depression

One view of childhood depression is that it is different from adult depression. According to this view, the symptoms are "masked"; that is, the depression is shown through behaviors and signs that are not necessarily associated with or thought to be related to depression. The idea behind masked depression is that the depressed feelings are replaced by behavioral problems.[1] Although there is some conflict around this idea, we believe that there is enough reason to consider some behaviors as possible masked depressive behaviors. These behaviors may be aggressive and negative, or the youth may be increasingly agitated. Such children may also complain frequently of physical aches and pains; their academic performance may decline, and they will have trouble paying attention and concentrating.

Aggressive or Negative Behaviors. The child will show generally aggressive or negative behavior both in and outside the home.

Possible Home Indicators. There are peer difficulties; your child may pick on siblings or friends. He or she may be aggressive, picking fights with others, and may be quick to react at the first hint of trouble. If your child is very verbal, he or she may talk back and may be verbally taunting or

abusive. The typical response to all interactions is negative
and perhaps even physical. Such children display disruptive
behavior both in and outside the home. They may yell, talk
back, and/or throw objects. It seems that these children or
adolescents seek any and every opportunity to challenge or
confront. They may even refuse punishment, and don't seem
to care about the consequences. They have a don't-care attitude about almost everything, which carries over into the
school setting. Because they are afraid of failing, most assignments are not done, much less started. Overall they
have a low tolerance for frustration, and lose control easily.

Increased Agitation. The child's overall physical activity is
increased; he or she cannot sit still. The youth is over-
involved and has difficulty completing any task or job.

Possible Home Indicators. Your child or adolescent may
have a short attention span, may be restless or easily distracted, and may be unable to sit still. He or she cannot deal
easily with frustration and reacts quickly, either verbally or
physically. Such children have difficulty staying on task and
have several projects going at once, but seldom complete any
of them. Often they don't hear directions, instructions, or
suggestions, and insist that they were never given. Frequently they ask unnecessary questions and/or make unnecessary comments. They often say the wrong thing at the
wrong time because of a lack of attention. These children
may speak or make noises at inappropriate times, talk back,
or mutter under their breath.

Increased Physical Aches, Pains, and Complaints. The child
or adolescent frequently complains of not feeling well.

Possible Home Indicators. Headaches, stomachaches, sore
muscles, and/or vague complaints of just not feeling well are
frequent. At school, these youths make frequent visits to the
school nurse or health aide. They may lie around the house,
saying they don't feel well. They seek constant attention,
but don't demand it. At times, the child may look like a lost

puppy and may follow the parent around continuously. These children lack attention and concentration. They may miss school frequently because of their vague physical complaints.

Declining Academic Performance. The child or adolescent is functioning below expected grade level.

Possible Home Indicators. Typically, independent work and homework assignments are poorly done. These children perform poorly on tests, not only because of lack of preparation but also because of inattentiveness. They either dawdle over the work or finish too quickly. They appear disorganized; work and desk are messy. Such children avoid responsibility, "forget" assignments and supplies, fall behind, and become overwhelmed. They are indecisive, and have a limited attention span and poor concentration. There may be a drop in grades; an A or B student may now earn Cs or Ds.

Poor Attention and Concentration. The child or adolescent cannot attend to tasks or focus his or her attention appropriately.

Possible Home Indicators. Your child takes an unusually long time to finish anything, or finishes quickly; in the latter case the work is poorly done. Behavior is disruptive because of an inability to stay with any task. Frequent guidance is necessary because the child misses directions. These youths have an excessive need for attention from parents and from siblings, teachers, and peers. They waste time with frequent dawdling. School materials, school assignments, and school and home responsibilities are forgotten. As a result they fall farther behind in class and work assignments every day. They frequently do nothing at home except watch TV or listen to the stereo. Excessive daydreaming may be noted.

Although these signs of depression may fit all children and adolescents at one time or another, it is the change in behaviors and the duration of that behavior that are important. If any abrupt change occurs in the child and if this change lasts approximately two weeks or longer, it would be wise to consult a mental health professional for evaluation and help.

Signals of Depression

1. Lack of interest
2. Change in appetite
3. Change in sleep pattern
4. Loss of energy
5. Blaming oneself inappropriately
6. Negative feelings about self
7. Feelings of sadness, hopelessness, and worry
8. Inability to concentrate or pay attention
9. Morbid thoughts
10. Aggressive or negative behaviors
11. Increased agitation
12. Increased physical aches, pains, and complaints
13. Declining academic performance
14. Poor attention and concentration

6

My Child—Suicide?

RECOGNIZING when your child or adolescent is at risk for a suicide is difficult because many of the symptoms sound like common behaviors for this age group. The youth at risk pushes erratic behavior to the extreme.

This chapter will list and discuss the signals of suicide and will specify what to look for. Although the signals of suicide and depression overlap, it is important to keep in mind that there is no one complete list for any child or adolescent, whether for depression or for suicide. Suicide is never due to anything as simple as a single cause. It is usually caused by a very complicated combination of social, emotional, and personal factors, to which may be added biological factors.

Suicide Warning List for Children and Adolescents

A Previous Suicide Attempt. Any previous attempt at suicide is a signal that some intervention should be undertaken.

Possible Home Indicators. A suicide attempt is any act or action that could possibly lead to death. These attempts range from the more obvious acts such as hanging, gunshot wounds, overdosing, asphyxiation, and knife wounds to the less obvious attempts such as anorexia, bulimia, carving initials into one's body, and substance abuse.

A Threat of Suicide. Such statements as "I'm going to kill myself," "I can't take it anymore," or "People would be better off without me" should be taken seriously, and the reason for such statements should be investigated. These are statements of extreme frustration and concern signaling a loss of hope, possibly with no way to turn except suicide.

Possible Home Indicators. A parent hearing these types of statements should discuss them with the child. Often young people convey their feelings and thoughts in journal writings, diaries, or letters, as well as in drawings. Any over-depressing or morbid writings or drawings should be investigated with your child. Any concern that your child or adolescent is experiencing stress or problems should be followed by contact with an appropriate mental health specialist.

Depression. Depression, as noted earlier, is not the occasional up-and-down mood that most children and adults experience at one time or another. Depression can be exhibited in a number of ways. It can follow the adult pattern, in which the person shows typical signs of depression, or it can be masked by behavioral problems. Depression is a serious illness that warrants investigation and intervention.

Possible Home Indicators. Changes in behavior that may be signs of depression should be seen for at least two weeks to allow for normal variations of mood cycles. Some of the warning signs are a lack of interest, change in appetite and/or sleep patterns, in which the child eats or sleeps more or less than usual, and a general loss of energy. You may also see negative feelings about self-worth and feelings of sadness, hopelessness, and worry, as well as an inability to concentrate and pay attention. Morbid thoughts, blaming oneself inappropriately, and a tendency to withdraw may also be seen.

Masked depression can be expressed as boredom, restlessness, fatigue, problems with attention and concentration, or complaints of illness, as well as general behavior problems. Many of the so-called acting-out behaviors could be signs of depression.

Feelings of Hopelessness and Helplessness. Often children and adolescents lead lives or encounter situations that are basically detrimental to their mental health. Because they are sometimes powerless to change or influence the course of their life or to resolve specific circumstances, they develop an overwhelming feeling of hopelessness. Seeing no resolution to their problems, they turn to suicide as a solution.

Possible Home Indicators. Children and adolescents with these feelings appear withdrawn, inhibited, and fearful; they look and feel unhappy. They give up easily and do not become involved because they feel powerless to influence anything. Frequent comments are "I can't," "It doesn't matter," "What difference does it make?" and "Why bother?" These children and adolescents develop "tunnel vision"; they can see only one solution to their problem, usually suicide. They fail to take into consideration any alternative solutions, even when these are offered to them.

Talk of Death or Despair, or a Preoccupation with Thoughts of Death. This symptom indicates that death has become a strong, perhaps frightening, force in their thinking pattern. Youths with this symptom need to have someone with whom they can share their concerns and who can help in breaking the thought pattern.

Possible Home Indicators. Any unusual interest in death, as evidenced through discussions and/or papers, themes, artwork, music, posters, or poems, should be of concern and should be discussed with your child and/or with appropriate mental health personnel. One type of theme that many people overlook as a suicide indicator is an overinvolvement with thoughts of war, terrorism, and/or suicide missions.

Anxiety and Tension. Although anxiety and tension are symptoms of many behavior patterns, they are of more serious consequence in suicide, especially if a parent sees them together with other signs.

Possible Home Indicators. Obvious signs of stress and tension are exhibited by little patience with self or others, withdrawal from usual social contacts, lowered school performance (as in poorly done assignments or poor test results), or poor attention and concentration. These children may argue more frequently with brothers and/or sisters or with you, the parents. They may also show less tolerance for their own mistakes and the mistakes of others. They are quickly angered, take longer to get over their anger, and are easily frustrated.

Withdrawal from Family and from Friends. While some children and adolescents act out their unhappiness so it can be seen, others withdraw into themselves, slowly cutting themselves off from everyone. Often they withdraw from family because of guilt or anger over their feelings and behaviors or simply because of their negative self-concept. They don't wish to burden their family or friends with their feelings and problems. These children and adolescents often fear getting angry, perhaps for fear of losing control. Suppressing this anger simply intensifies it until finally they act on it, often by suicide. We feel that these are the youths at greatest risk, who need to be reached quickly.

Possible Home Indicators. Your child may exhibit quiet, withdrawn behavior that was not previously present. He or she participates less in family discussions, and avoids groups and group participation. The youth may procrastinate; homework assignments are poorly done, if they are done at all. Poor attention and concentration are apparent. If questioned, he or she will make up any kind of excuse, usually "I forgot" or "I don't know." These youths may appear to be daydreaming or off in another world. Physical movements are slowed down. Sometimes it even appears to be an effort to leave the house.

Violent or Rebellious Behavior. Some children and adolescents act out their feelings rather than trying to resolve them by dealing with them constructively. They simply get rid of any feelings they have through acting out. They may be involved in petty crimes, act violent, run away from home or school, or involve themselves in generally antisocial behavior as a way of coping with their feelings. Acting-out behaviors are often seen as normal, especially for boys, but the extent and magnitude may signal a loss of control such as that seen in suicide.

Possible Home Indicators. Acting-out behaviors can be demonstrated both verbally and physically. These children may abuse you or their brothers and sisters, verbally or physically. There may be theft and lack of respect for others or their property. Often they respond negatively to authority. They may appear to be overactive, and may pester or pick on you or other family members or friends. These youths interrupt others, and may be loud and obnoxious. They have no delay mechanism on behavior, so they may try to satisfy all desires immediately, perhaps even crudely. At school they may write on desks, tear pages out of books, or mutilate equipment and lockers. They appear to be withdrawn or "out of it." These children don't smile or laugh, and appear to be angry at the world. They may have a "chip on the shoulder" attitude. Overall they are inattentive and fidgety.

Drug and Alcohol Abuse. Drugs and alcohol abuse is seen by some as a slow form of suicide. Certainly it is a signal of a young person's inability to cope with the stresses of reality. All too often, these youths withdraw into themselves. Many adolescents who commit suicide used drugs or alcohol shortly before their death; a large amount of alcohol or drugs lessens the fear of death. In addition, alcohol and drugs often make them more aggressive. If this aggression is turned inward toward themselves instead of outward toward others, suicide may be the result.[1]

Possible Home Indicators. Under the influence of drugs or alcohol, young people can show either withdrawn or acting-out behaviors. They lack attention and concentration or, as some youths say, they "mellow out." Also, their mood may be unusually high or low. Depending on the substance used, they may have red eyes, dilated pupils, sniffles, a runny nose, or hoarseness. Their appearance may become sloppier; their behavior may become more careless. They may steal from home as well as from other places. These young people may sell personal or family belongings; Often they claim to have lost or misplaced them, or to have lent them to a friend.

Giving Away Valued Possessions or Making "Final Arrangements." These are usually more apparent signs that a young person may be thinking about suicide. Final arrangements can take various forms, such as giving away valued possessions or making a will, which is given to a "good friend" to hold.

Possible Home Indicators. Any suggestion from your child or adolescent, or from their friends, that they are making final arrangements should result in some discussion and possibly in contact with an appropriate mental health professional. Giving away valued tapes, CDs, records, books, pictures, posters, clothes, money, or any other valued possession should be investigated. Notes left "hidden" in hopes of being found, which talk about death or suicide, are often cries for intervention.

Abrupt Changes in Behavior. Changes in mood are not unexpected in children and adolescents, or in adults, but abrupt and prolonged changes in behavior may be cause for concern. Usually there are reasons why someone goes from being happy to being moody, from outgoing behavior to withdrawal, from being passive to being aggressive, and from concern to lack of concern. These reasons may be temporary and transient, or serious enough to be a factor in suicide.

Possible Home Indicators. Look for behaviors that are the opposite of what is expected from your child. For example, be alert to behavior that was previously outgoing but now is withdrawn. Previously your child or adolescent may have chatted easily with you, siblings, teachers, and friends, but now he or she avoids even the most casual contact. Once interested in various activities, he or she may now show a lack of involvement in anything. Another example is the shy or quiet youngster who suddenly becomes openly hostile or aggressive. This change should always be investigated.

Sudden, Unexplained "High" or Whirlwind Activity after a Period of Depression. This change could mean that the child has decided to take the fatal step. Indecision about whether or not to kill oneself often contributes to tension, anxiety, and depression. Once a child or an adolescent has made a decision, either positive or negative, these feelings lessen somewhat. In some cases the decision may have been made to commit suicide, and the child feels relief over having made that decision.

Possible Home Indicators. After a period of withdrawn or "down" behavior, your child or adolescent suddenly becomes talkative, excited, and sometimes boisterous and loud. Young people in this state, who were once able to control themselves, now cannot sit still or concentrate. There is a constant fiddling with any object that comes to hand. They may begin one activity or job, only to begin another quickly without ever finishing the first, or they may rush through with many careless errors.

Running Away from Home. Children and adolescents give a variety of reasons for running away from home. Usually the reasons are legitimate in their minds; they range from what they see as unfair restrictions to serious abuse. Running away suggests some problems within the family as well as within the child or adolescent. Often running away is seen as a last resort; it also serves notice that the young person finds the situation at home or at school intolerable. If the situation is not resolved at least to some degree, the child or adolescent may see no way out but suicide.

Possible Home Indicators. Some real or even imagined crises at home or at school may cause running away. Typically the runaways have lower grades, higher absenteeism, and difficulty in interacting with teachers and peers. They also show less involvement with extracurricular school activities.[2] Within the home, such children or adolescents show less interest and involvement in family affairs and activities.

Change in School and Academic Performance. Most children and adolescents do not function consistently in school. They have normal highs and lows, successes and failures. They like some subjects and dislike others. Changes in school and academic performance among children who have a high degree of concern seem to affect their general functioning and usually occur over a period of time. A usually good student begins to fail; he or she misses school more often; assignments are late or poorly done or are not handed in at all; and his or her attitude toward school becomes negative. These are signs that the child or adolescent doesn't care. They are preoccupied with other thoughts or with things of greater priority. Other issues need to be resolved. Taken to an extreme and coupled with other factors, suicide may be a way of dealing with all of their failures, especially among learning-disabled students. A pilot study of fourteen suicide victims in Los Angeles County found that 50 percent were learning disabled.[3]

Possible Home Indicators. Grades and performance usually deteriorate, and the quality of work declines. Your child's attitude toward school, if not negative, is passive; he or she doesn't care, and is absent frequently. The student seems to be easily distracted and displays a loss of interest. Overall there is poor attention and concentration.

Boredom. Boredom is still a possible factor in suicide. Most people go through periods of boredom from time to time, but it may deserve concern when it becomes the rule rather than the exception. It would seem in this age of electronics and computers that there are ample activities to keep children and adolescents from becoming bored; their lives are filled with one activity after another. Yet in spite of all there is to stimulate the mind and body, children and adolescents frequently complain of being bored; many expect someone or something to entertain them. Perhaps boredom is a factor in the increased use of drugs and alcohol in our adolescent populations, and may also account in part for the epidemic of teenage pregnancies. At any rate, seeing children and adolescents in a constant state of boredom when there is so much to stimulate them suggests withdrawal or inability to adjust to life in general. Being out of step with peers has been a factor in more than a few suicides.

Possible Home Indicators. Not only is your child easily distracted, but he or she distracts others as well. Responsibilities are met quickly or not at all, or are forgotten. Often these young people forget to do their homework, fail to complete projects, or forget to bring materials and books to school. There may be an attitude of "Do whatever you like. It doesn't matter to me." They don't accept responsibility. Along with poor attention and concentration, they display restlessness. They may be involved in drugs or alcohol, with some noticeable reaction at home.

Inability to Concentrate. The ability to concentrate depends on one's capacity to focus on one train of thought without other thoughts interfering. Children and adolescents who are upset enough to consider suicide are constantly dealing with and attempting to analyze many thoughts and feelings related to how they feel about themselves. Because of the hurt and pain they feel, they are often dealing with conflicting feelings and emotions, trying to put everything into focus. It is impossible for them to focus and concentate on any one issue, especially academics, because their attempts to deal with their emotions take a higher priority.

Possible Home Indicators. Your adolescent or child may become a daydreamer. He or she may be easily distracted, inattentive, and often late for school or appointments. If responsibilities are completed, they are rushed through and are not done very well. These youths have trouble getting started on almost anything. They are frequently disorganized and need help.

Because they are thinking about so many things, they are often seen as "forgetful," especially about responsibilities. When questioned about the "forgetfulness" they usually say "Sorry," with no explanation. Some children or adolescents seem to develop an extreme need to depend on others.

Feelings of Worthlessness. Many children and adolescents who think of suicide have feelings of worthlessness and perhaps hatred for themselves. They measure themselves against significant people in their lives and usually fall short. They magnify their weaknesses and avoid emphasizing their strengths because they don't recognize or believe they have any strengths. Some children and adolescents who have these feelings may try to cover them up so that no one else will know that they're "not any good."

Possible Home Indicators. You may see withdrawn behavior and a lack of confidence. Your child may cry easily and react strongly to even the slightest criticism. Typically, schoolwork is poorly done. If asked to make corrections, the child may ignore the request or may even repeat the same errors. Socially, these youths may tend to associate with younger children. Sometimes they become upset both physically and mentally because they fret too much and become moody. These children have difficulty with change in a routine and cannot handle surprises easily.

Those children and adolescents who try to cover up their feelings of worthlessness may attempt to make themselves look superior by making others look inferior. Other possible cover-up tactics are sarcasm, attention-seeking behavior, or behavior that at first might be regarded as competitive but at a second look is more imposing and challenging. The child may laugh and talk at inappropriate times.

Physical Complaints. Children and adolescents with chronic illnesses are probably more prone to depression than average. Children without chronic illnesses who are depressed often complain of vague physical symptoms that cannot be verified or diagnosed.

Possible Home Indicators. You will hear frequent complaints of minor aches and pains, frequent requests at school to visit the nurse, and frequent tardiness and absences. Older children and adolescents may openly "self-doctor"; they may take aspirin or over-the-counter medication frequently and make a show of it. Younger children may follow you around frequently, asking you to look at small scratches, scrapes, and bumps. At times, a younger child may follow you around continuously. You may even be unaware that the child is there until you look up and find him or her beside you.

Changes in Sleeping Patterns. Changes in children's and adolescents' sleeping habits may be seen in different ways. They may start sleeping for longer periods of time or may not sleep much at all; they may not sleep at regular times but at odd hours. Sleep may also be easily disturbed, so the end result is exhaustion. Over a period of time, this pattern may result in physical and/or psychological problems because natural defenses have been weakened.

Possible Home Indicators. Your child may complain of being tired and sleepy. Some youths may even fall asleep during class, and the teacher may have difficulty waking them. They may frequently miss classes and school because of oversleeping. Achievement falls because they have missed so much class and school. When present in class, they may not know what's going on.

At home, these children fall asleep watching television or doing homework. They have obvious difficulty in paying attention and concentrating, possibly accompanied by restlessness. They seldom take care of their responsibilities or chores, and show very little energy. These young people choose to stay inside the house after school rather than going out to play; they are just plain tired.

Recent Suicide of Someone Close or Someone with Whom Child Identifies. It is presently thought that a person is more likely to commit suicide if there has been a suicide in his or her family. Also, those who are already contemplating suicide may be encouraged to complete it by the suicide of someone they know, like, or admire. Because children and adolescents identify so closely with friends as well as with popular personalities from movies and television shows, suicide by any of these people may bring them closer to making their own attempt. Often suicide victims are glamorized by their schools and by the media. This treatment affects others who are fragile and vulnerable; they view the recognition and attention obtained by suicide as very appealing.

Possible Home Indicators. Your child or adolescent focuses too much on the morbid and the depressing, with references to death. Although this overfocusing can occur almost anywhere, English teachers in particular often receive clues about suicidal youths in their creative writings and in discussions. There is notably poor attention and concentration.

Changes in Eating Habits. The present emphasis on physical fitness can be expected to influence children and adolescents and their eating habits. Within limits, this situation is normal, but serious eating disorders such as bulimia and anorexia nervosa or periods of starvation and binge eating are certainly problem signs. Any sudden change in eating patterns should be cause for concern.

Possible Home Indicators. There is either avoidance of food or overinvolvement with food. Your child may not eat snacks, breakfast, or lunch, or may consume his or hers and help others finish their food. Those youths who are avoiding food may be giving most of their food away. Those who are overconcerned with food will hide, hoard, and/or steal food. Again, attention and concentration in general are poor.

Abrupt Changes in School Attendance. Parents, along with school officials, need to be alert to students with an average to good school attendance record who begin to show excessive absences. A common situation before a suicide is involvement in a school-related crisis.[4,5]

Possible Home Indicators. Those with an average to good attendance record begin abruptly to show excessive absenteeism. When questioned, they have countless reasons for missing school, such as being sick, oversleeping, or parents needing them at home. Achievement declines because they miss so much school. When they are in school, often they are so far behind that it is impossible to catch up on the work. They are unaware of what is going on in the classroom. Although they are present in body, these children are mentally absent.

In conclusion, although most people who attempt or complete suicide give signs of their intention, they may give different signs to different people, thereby never allowing one person to put all the signs together. This fact emphasizes the importance of acting on any sign from children and adolescents that they may be thinking about suicide.

Signals of Suicide

A Previous Suicide Attempt

A Threat of Suicide

Depression

Feelings of Hopelessness and Helplessness

Talk of Death or Despair, or a Preoccupation with Thoughts of Death

Anxiety and Tension

Withdrawal from Family and from Friends

Violent or Rebellious Behavior

Drug or Alcohol Abuse

Giving Away Valued Possessions or Making Final Arrangements

Abrupt Changes in Behavior

Sudden, Unexplained High or Whirlwind Activity after a Period of Depression

Runnning Away from Home

Change in School and Academic Performance

Boredom

Inability to Concentrate

Feelings of Worthlessness

Physical Complaints

Changes in Sleeping Patterns

Recent Suicide of Someone Close or Someone with Whom They Identify

Changes in Eating Habits

Abrupt Changes in School Attendance

7

Stress

STRESS affects chidren and adults alike. Many adults, however, do not understand how children feel and respond to stress. Perhaps an example will help you understand.

You and your spouse find that you are expecting another baby. You are both pleased, and lovingly tell your five-year-old child that because you are so pleased and happy with him or her, you are going to have another baby. Of course you expect the child to be as happy as you are about the coming event.

Now let's change things around a little and see how you would react to a similar situation. Your spouse comes to you and says, "Honey, you are such a great wife (husband) and I'm so happy with you that I'm going to bring home another woman (man) to share our life." Would you be as pleased as your spouse?

Most children probably don't know what stress is all about. They hear the word and listen to adults discuss it, but to them it may simply be the end result of a situation that leaves them feeling bad. Adolescents see stress as being caused by the demands placed on them by parents and teachers. These demands may be normal and expected, but because of their nature and frequency, stress is often the result. The demands are called stressors; the response to such demands is stress.

Because stressors are demands made on people, they can often be pleasant experiences, but usually stress is seen as bad. For children and adolescents, stress has been related to medical problems, social and emotional problems, and delinquent behavior. The effects of stress differ from one person to another, and each person will probably develop his or her own way of handling stress. Some environments—like home and school—are more stressful than others, thus increasing the pressure on all involved. Also, stress is cumulative and progressive; that is, it piles up and grows worse as it continues. Fortunately, the ability to recognize stress and to deal with it improves with age and intellectual growth.[1]

Stress is a normal reaction. It is only when stress can't be handled that it may cause physical or emotional problems. How a child or adolescent handles stress probably depends on his or her perception of self and of the stressful experience. The perception of self would be as one who does or does not have the ability, power, or control needed to avoid or minimize a stressful event. The perception of the stressful event would be whether it could have been avoided or minimized.

Some children cope well with stress. These children believe in themselves as competent people; their confidence in themselves grows with each success.

Most children, however, have to work at coping with stress. They may or may not be able to see and handle it as part of life. Their success in dealing with stress is not as frequent as among the children mentioned above, so their experience with stress grows more slowly. There are also children who cope with stress very poorly. These children have great difficulty in dealing with any stressful experience. Their lack of success leads them to believe that they can't handle stress; this belief in turn causes them to deal with it poorly. The basis of a child's ability or lack of ability to cope is not fully understood.[2] Children who cope poorly are more prone to depression and suicide.

Children who use various types of strategies to avoid the causes of tension in their lives receive only short-term benefits. Those children who are able to acknowledge and accept the stress, however, are emotionally and even physically healthier. Basically there are four ways to avoid stress: denial, regression, withdrawal, and impulsive acting out.[3]

Denial. In denial, the child or adolescent acts as if nothing has happened. If the stressful event is ignored, perhaps there will be no pain; the event will disappear and life will go on as before. Joey was a preschooler who had recently lost his father. When told of his father's death, he continued to play with his cars and trucks. He never asked any questions relating to his father's death, but on occasion he made comments implying that his father was just away.

Regression. With regression, children or adolescents under stress act younger than their years. They become dependent and demanding. Younger children may return to thumb sucking, bed-wetting, temper tantrums, or other childish habits. When Mark's father, who is in the U.S. Navy, leaves home for sea duty, Mark regresses. His behaviors become more childish than those of the typical twelve-year-old boy. He whines, clings more to his mother, refuses to participate in his usual sports activities, and occasionally wets the bed.

Withdrawal. In withdrawal, stressed children or adolescents remove themselves from the situation either physically or mentally. They seem almost to disappear. They might be overattentive to pets and/or inanimate objects. Daydreaming increases. When Keri's mother was hospitalized for the third and final time, Keri's typical sixteen-year-old behavior, spending time in her room listening to music, increased dramatically. Her favorite activity, talking on the phone, decreased; she gradually cut herself off from her close friends. Even when she was with the rest of the family, Keri said little and kept to herself.

Acting Out. When children or adolescents display impulsive acting-out behavior, they are trying to avoid thinking about the past and/or about the consequences of their behavior. They cover up their feelings by making others angry at them. Of all the ways that children or adolescents use to avoid a stress, this method is perhaps the most destructive. Eighteen-year-old Jim was a star basketball player in high school who had hopes of playing in college and perhaps professionally. After injuring himself in a game, he was seen by an orthopedic surgeon. The injury was minor, but during the workup the surgeon found a degenerative condition that ended Jim's basketball career. His depression was so over-whelming that he began to argue and fight with his parents as well as with his friends. He began drinking and staying out late; at times he didn't come home until late morning or afternoon.

There are also positive ways that children and adolescents use to handle stress.[4] These ways include altruism, joking, suppression and involvement in other activities, anticipa-tion, and sublimation. Remember, however, that these posi-tive stress-reducing strategies, if carried to an extreme, can become negative.

Altruism. One strategy is the use of altruism. Helping oth-ers, especially parents, lets the children or adolescents focus less on their own troubles, and gives them satisfaction and the knowledge that they are useful. When Mary's mother was hospitalized, she not only did the cooking for the family but also began to volunteer as a candy striper at the hospi-tal.

Joking. Joking is a way of expressing pain, hurt, and anger. Keith, crippled in an auto accident, began to draw cartoon characters in wheelchairs and developed a portfolio of his work.

Suppression and Involvement in Other Activities. These strategies allow children or adolescents to regain their bal-ance. It gives them breathing space; they are able to return to the stressful event when they are ready. Six-year-old Sally accepted the news of her mother's death with tears and sad-ness. Later in the day she played house with her dolls, and went to be held and comforted by her father when she began to think about her mother. Days after the funeral, Sally played "funeral" with her dolls; in this way she played out her unhappiness and grief.

Anticipation. This is one of the better coping strategies used by children and adolescents. When they learn from one stressful event, they can foresee and plan for the next. Michael had recently flunked a major test, which threatened his class standing and future scholarship hopes. He had felt that he could breeze through the test with little studying. Knowing that another major test could make or break his scholarship chances, Michael set aside extra time for his studies and took more care with his note taking.

Sublimation. When we sublimate, we expresss our feelings through unrelated activities, as when children or adolescents become heavily involved in games, sports, or hobbies. In this way they can express their hurts, pain, fears, and anger in a socially acceptable manner. Doug, after breaking up with his girlfriend, devoted long hours to practicing his golf game.

Families also differ in the extent to which they help children develop coping skills. Children who cope well come from families where parents are warm, loving, and supportive, and communicate well. These parents encourage independence but have strong convictions about right and wrong. They explain their reasons for their expectations and insist on proper behavior.[5,6] It is important to understand that no one type of parenting style enables coping skills to develop in children.[7] The traits listed above, however, should be woven into any parenting style. It should also be recognized that friends and relatives as well as environmental factors play a part in developing coping skills. Because these factors cannot be controlled, it falls upon the family to be as supportive as possible.

Most parents recognize the stress that results from major stressors such as death, divorce, unemployment, drug and alcohol abuse, and serious illness. These will be discussed later. Parents and people in general, however, do not recognize the stresses that arise from common events. Parents see these events either as minor or as a normal part of life and thus of no serious or lasting consequence. To the child or adolescent, however, some of these common events could be major stressors. Many such events involve school and their peer group. Children from about age six to age eleven fear being upset over events at school. They fear being rejected or embarrassed by peers, being sent to the principal's office, or not being promoted. All of these situations, and others, can place tremendous pressure on children.

For children in preadolescent to early adolescent years, aged eleven to fifteen, school-related problems cause much of the stress. These children are very much concerned with school performance whether they are A students or failing all subjects. Adolescents in general see examinations, career choices, sex, and peer pressure to use drugs or alcohol as major stressors.[8] They also feel serious stress from losses of any kind, not only those caused by death, divorce, separation, or family relocation. Many react strongly to the losses discussed in the chapter on depression, namely loss of childhood, loss of familiar boundaries and guidelines, loss of an ideal body image, loss of self-esteem, or loss of goals.

Major Stressors

A catastrophe is something that happens unexpectedly and causes fear and stress in all involved. A family either finds the strength to deal with a catastrophe or falls apart. Those who are able to deal with it will put aside minor individual differences and unite to deal with the crisis. Those who fall apart will attempt to deal with the event as individuals without seeking support from others and without the inner resources to cope. Regardless of the source of stress, family members will encounter more arguing, tension, fighting with other family members, problems in eating and sleeping, and minor physical complaints.

Stress comes from many sources when unexpected events occur. There is little or no time to prepare. Families are unable to plan and put into action any type of survival program. Usually they have little, if any, previous experience, so they don't know what to expect. The results of crisis are often long-lasting, so that the stress is prolonged. A crisis or a catastrophe also brings a sense of loss, whether through death or through the loss of ability to function or cope. The disruption—even the destruction—of a family and of its life-style is quite possible. Stress is also very high when one or more family members are threatened or put into danger of any sort. The emotional impact is immediate, and may result in such reactions as depression, and eating or sleeping disorders; and it is long-lasting, possibly resulting in social withdrawal and interpersonal confusion. Stress also leaves its mark through medical problems, which in turn result in more stress. Problems such as headache, hypertension, heart disease, and skin disorders may be common.[9]

Some (but by no means all) of the serious catastrophic events that families may encounter are death, divorce, unemployment, drug or alcohol abuse, and serious illness. These events lead to stress; stress may lead to depression; depression may lead to suicide.

Death

Death is by far the greatest tragedy that families experience. The amount of stress depends on whether the death is sudden or follows a prolonged illness. When the death is sudden, families are unprepared; their resources for coping are taxed. When the death is expected and comes after a long illness, the immediate stress may be less, but it was continuous while the loved one was ill. The amount of stress felt at the death of a family member also depends on how much stress exists from other sources. The stress of death is compounded by making arrangements and by dealing with all the professional persons necessary in settling the estate.

The grief and stress among children and adolescents follow those of adults, for the most part. How these feelings are handled makes the difference between a good and a poor adjustment. A poor adjustment could be a contributing factor in depression and suicide. Perhaps of greatest importance is that adults recognize children's right and need to grieve. Too often, however, they become so involved in their own grief that they don't give consideration to the children's needs. Along with the recognition of a child's grief, adults need to give children time to accept and understand the loss. They need to discuss death in realistic terms with their children and to let them know how they, as adults, feel and cope. They need to allow children to express themselves and their understanding of what happened. Most of all, they need to listen to the children and to respect what they say.[10]

Research on separation and attachment suggests that children are able to confront and work through their losses if the following circumstances exist:

1. There has been a secure relationship with the parents before the loss.
2. Information is accurate and quickly given; questions are answered honestly.
3. The youth is allowed to mourn and grieve the loss with the family. In cases of a loss through death, the youth chooses to participate as much or as little as he or she wishes with regard to the funeral rites.
4. There is a continuing relationship with a significant person whom the youth trusts.[11]

Suggestions. An excellent book for parents or for any adult who is confronted with helping children to deal with a loss is *Helping Children Cope with Separation and Loss*, by C. Jewett.[12] Conversations or activities with your child or adolescent should be kept brief. Maintain the usual routines as much as possible. Answer your child's questions as honestly as you can. In talking to your child about a loss, start with his or her experiences with the person: "You may have noticed that Daddy's not been home very much lately" or "Remember when Mommy was in the hospital. . ." When you begin a conversation by using your child's observations or experiences, it's harder for them to deny their thoughts and feelings.[13] When talking about a loss in this way, your child or adolescent begins to develop a sense of competency or trust about his or her own observations. Use nonverbal communications (holding, touching, or rocking) to convey the feeling that your child is not alone. Share the sadness; remember both the good and the bad times spent with the dead person. Put together a photo or scrapbook. Reassure your child that hurting is a natural part of the grieving process and will lessen with time. Encourage your child or adolescent to draw, write, and play out how he or she feels.

Divorce

Divorce is a serious source of stress not only for the parents but also for the children. Perhaps the only event that causes greater stress is death, but then divorce can be seen as the death of a highly emotional relationship. A number of factors determine how children will adjust to divorce:

1. How nurturing the relationship is between the children and the parent who receives custody;
2. The quality of the relationship between father and mother after divorce;
3. The emotional adjustment of the parent, especially the one with custody;
4. A reasonable and reliable relationship with the parent who doesn't have custody;
5. Financial condition;
6. The children's feeling of having some control of the divorce situation.[14,15]

The way children view divorce is related to how they understand this confusing idea. Children aged three to six years are very personal in their thinking. Their concept of love relies on the amount of physical distance between themselves and others. Therefore if a parent leaves the house, it's because the child is no longer loved or liked. The explanation "Daddy didn't leave you, he left Mommy" is not understood. The child equates his or her behavior with what has happened: "I must have done something bad to cause Daddy to go away and not like me anymore."

Children aged five to eight years still are personal in their thinking, but now can see conflicts between their mother and their father. Like the younger children, however, they view their own behavior as the determining cause of a divorce. If the parents fought, it's because of something they did. This idea reinforces the belief that their parent's divorce can be "fixed." If they were bad, they can be good, and their parents can be married again. In addition to their sense of responsibility for the divorce, children of this age also feel responsible for keeping the noncustodial parent happy. If the noncustodial parent does not visit, the child feels that he or she could not please or make that parent happy. These children always fear that the noncustodial parent will find another little girl or boy to love.

Children aged nine to twelve years can see their parents as having feelings that can change. They still tend to oversimplify the situation within the home, however, believing that everything would be all right if their parents would only try harder.[16]

In order to minimize the amount of stress on children, parents must give the children an explanation of the divorce that the children can understand. This explanation will put the situation in perspective for them and will prevent the possiblity that the child or children will assume responsibility or blame for the divorce. It is important that the explanation of the divorce fit the child's age level. Children, especially those who have a poor self-image and poor coping skills, will need the emotional support of both parents. There is a very strong relationship between how the parents, especially the one with custody, adjust to the divorce and how the children adjust. One certainly cannot expect a good or less stressful adjustment when the parents are angry and hostile toward one another and when they use the children as a way of getting even with the ex-spouse. Nor can one expect children to cope with the divorce when there are insufficient finances, when they are forced to relocate both home and school, or when they must adjust to new and different people, with whom their parents will now associate.[17]

Suggestions. As soon as possible, talk to your child or adolescent about issues that are important to him or her and that will affect the acceptance of the divorce. These issues include the following: "Where will I (mother, father) live?" "Can I visit the parent who is leaving?" "Who will take care of me?" "Will there be money enough for us?" "Do we have to move?" "What about the pets?" Talking to a trusted adult helps. If there is any fighting between the parents, ask your child or adolescent to leave the room. Encourage your child to keep a journal of feelings, (anger, fear, sadness), to write a poem, or to draw a picture.

Unemployment

In this age, when both parents must work to make ends meet, unemployment by one or both parents could be a major source of stress. Children especially respond to parental unemployment with ambivalence. While they resent the loss of money, they also want to help, and may even see themselves as somehow making everything OK again.

Children, especially adolescents, identify more and more closely with a peer culture that emphasizes material goods. The loss of ability to keep up with their friends causes stress. Often other family members are required to work when the main wage earner is unemployed. Adolescents in particular may be upset because working upsets their education or their social life. They may see the unemployed wage earner as a failure; this view causes stress in their relationship with that person. •If the wife was working as a homemaker and must now become employed, stress can result from the disruption that children feel, or from the fact that the husband may not assume the household duties. Cutting back on everything except necessities results in fewer social opportunities. Reduction of social opportunities means less support from friends and peers. Staying home results in boredom and possibly in anger and hostility toward the person or persons who caused the situation.

Suggestions. Explain to your children or adolescents how the job loss will affect his or her life. They may want to help; talking to them about ways to do this, such as babysitting or cutting grass, is important for their sense of well-being.

Alcohol and/or Drug Abuse

Much has been written about the use of alcohol and drugs, not only by children and adolescents but also by adults. One could say that parents who use or abuse alcohol or drugs will probably find their children and adolescents using them. The overuse of prescription or nonprescription drugs for sleep, for relaxation, or just to feel good may also make parents unable to help and support a child or an adolescent who is using drugs. Stress therefore may be increased. Also, children and adolescents who reject a lack of closeness, support, and affection from their parents are more likely to begin and continue the use and abuse of drugs and/or alcohol.[18,19]

A number of family-related, stressful events occur within one year before the adolescent begins to use and abuse drugs and/or alcohol. These include increased arguments with parents, a change in the family's financial status, an increase in arguments between parents, the mother beginning to work outside the home, and the hospitalization of a parent. Other stressful events include a change in the father's occupation, the loss of a job by a parent, marital separation of parents, divorce, the marriage of a parent to a stepparent, a third adult in the family, a parent arrested and jailed, and the death of a sibling.[20]

Increased drug use by children and adolescents increases the possibility of suicide because it makes them less fearful of death, reduces inhibitions, and allows them to take more chances.

Suggestions. For any family member—adult, adolescent, or child—contact local agencies dealing with alcohol and drug abuse. They can provide both individual and group counseling and information on support groups such as Alcoholic Anonymous, Al-Anon, Alateen, Narcotics Anonymous, or Adult Children of Alcoholics. Talking to a trusted friend helps. Recognize that you can't control another person's drinking or drug use, but that there are people to help you.

Serious Illness

Serious illness, whether in a child, an adolescent, or an adult, creates great stress on all members of the family. It strains family relationships; tension and conflict increase because more time, energy, and possibly finances are required for the sick person. Family activities may be limited because options for social activities and leisure time are limited. There is an increase in the amount of time needed to care for the individual and in the number of related tasks that must be performed. Finances may become tight and perhaps even burdensome, so the needs and desires of others may not be met. Education or work may be interrupted or changed to fit the sick person's needs. If the illness is terminal, the anticipation of the death would certainly add more stress to that caused by the other factors mentioned.[21]

Suggestions. Maintain routines and family rules as much as possible. Explain the nature of the illness in terms that your child can understand; give as much information as necessary, and adapt it to his or her level. Reassure the child that he or she will be cared for; tell how this will occur. Accept and discuss the various feelings that your child or adolescent is experiencing. When a parent or a child is hospitalized, there is a period of preparation and adaptation. During these periods, emphasize who will be in charge and what reponsibilities each person will have. Maintain as much contact as possible with the hospitalized person. If the parent or child is separated from the family, display a photo of that person in a prominent place. It also helps the hospitalized person to have pictures from home.

One-Parent and Multiparent Families

One-parent and multiparent families share the same stresses as a two-parent family. They also have additional stresses, however, which are unique to their situation and to each family. In one-parent and multiparent families, extra adults might be present in the household. These could be the adult's own parents or grandparents, various relatives, or other unrelated persons such as girlfriends or boyfriends.

In one-parent families, the relationship between parent and child merges, and the child might be called upon to fulfill the departed spouse's role. He or she is asked to help make financial decisions, to give advice about dating, and to assume the role of confidant. There is a loss of role model.

In multiparent families, the child or adolescent must learn to deal with separate homes, multiple parents, (stepmother/biological father, stepfather/biological mother), as many as eight grandparents, various relatives such as aunts, uncles, and cousins, and possibly siblings, stepsiblings, and half-siblings. In many cases, there is more than one remarriage.

Adjusting to new relationships is a stress that is thrust upon the child or adolescent. He or she must give up the fantasy of the two parents reuniting; often little time is given to grieve the loss of the old family. New fears replace the old ones: "Will this marriage fail too?" "Do I have to call him (or her) Daddy (or Mommy)?" "Who's the boss?" New alliances are formed: "Will my real Daddy (or Mommy) love my new brother or sister more than me?" Stress is added when the new relationships remove children or adolescents from their biological sibling; one child goes with the father, another with the mother. Stress also occurs when a child becomes closer to a stepsibling than to the biological brother or sister. The new relationships also reflect position changes; the oldest child might be the middle or the youngest child in the new family. Along with the position change comes loss of status. It is difficult to go from being the oldest child to the middle or the youngest, or from being the baby in the family to babysitting for younger children.

If the relationships between the youth's two households are filled with anger and hostility, the youth's stress level increases as the involvement with each family increases.

With a remarriage, there is usually a move to a new home and neighborhood, a transfer to a new school, and a loss of friends. These changes can create resentment and anger against the new family and a longing for the old.

Children and adolescents who formerly could claim most of a parent's attention must now share their parent. It is even more stress-provoking when they see a parent as becoming too involved with the new spouse and his or her children.

Suggestions. Discuss specific issues with your child or adolescent. These issues concern family rules, terms of address (what the child calls the new parent), who has the right to discipline or punish, why the child's name is different from everyone else's, and the status of various members of the blended household. Maintain a routine for visits and events. Have a room or space available for your visiting child or adolescent, if possible. Discuss new schools, neighborhoods, and friends.

School Stresses

Our experience in the schools and with school-age children has led us to be concerned for a long time with the causes of stress in the classroom and in the school in general. Although stress in itself may not be bad, and although at times we all experience a high degree of stress, continued pressure on children from many sources could result in the breakdown of mental health, leading to depression and suicide.

Stress reactions involve the ego—that is, how a person sees his or her own personality or self. To protect the self, a person builds up a number of defenses as a way of dealing with stress. Children and adolescents react in the same manner, using some type of defense or reaction to lessen the stress and to keep the self free from threat. Many of the behaviors seen in children in school are reactions to real or perceived threats.

The way in which chidren and adolescents cope with stress is largely determined by their anxiety. Their reaction to anxiety is formed by two perceptions.

1. Did the child or teen have any power to reduce, avoid, or end a stressful event or situation, either real or imagined?
2. After the stressful event, were the resulting feelings positive in that the youth was able to "handle" the stress, or was he or she left with feelings of vulnerability and helplessness?[22]

When children and teens are unable to cope effectively and when stress continues, depression and (for some of the more vulnerable youths) suicidal behaviors result.

The complexity of the school and of classrooms is so great that it is impossible simply to identify stress and remove it. But if parents become aware of how the school contributes to their children's stress, perhaps they can find ways to reduce that stress so that their children's education can be a positive experience.

Some of the stressors that your children may experience are listed below by grade but not in order of priority. The suggestions that are given are global and can be applied whenever seen as necessary or useful. Remember that open communication, active listening, and establishing clear rules and expectations are always part of good parenting.

Kindergarten. Children at this age may fear riding the bus because they may miss their stop; the driver won't know where they live, or other kids on the bus may frighten them. They fear wetting themselves or becoming ill while in school. They also fear that they may be abandoned by their parents, who won't pick them up after school, that they will be forgotten, or that they will get home and their parents or significant adult won't be there.

Suggestions. Introduce your child to the school bus driver; assure the child that he or she will generally be protected on the bus. For children who are chronic wetters, leave a set of dry clothing with the school nurse. If a wetting accident occurs, assure them that you or someone will bring them dry clothing; accidents do happen, and they are to try not to worry about it. Tell them that if they get sick, there is a school nurse or aide who will take care of them and who will call you. Reassure children at this stage that they will not be abandoned; if ever you are not home, prepare them with advice about what to do. Make sure they have telephone numbers of people to call.

First Grade. First grade fears are similar to kindergarten fears, but children now seem to be more concerned with the teacher's approval or disapproval. They are also concerned with peer relationships and with being ridiculed.

Suggestions. Use some of the same suggestions presented above. Introduce yourself to your child's teacher and talk in positive terms to the child about the teacher. Your child will sense any criticism that you may have about the teacher or the school. Assure the child that his or her relationship with kids in school will not be much different from the relationship with present friends. Discuss social skills, expectations, and behaviors.

Second Grade. In the second grade, children become more concerned about how they fit in. Will they be perceived as different from all the other children? Will they look different from the other kids? The child also wants to be recognized and approved by the teacher; will he or she be chosen for a classroom job or errand? At this point children start to be concerned about their academic success. They begin to note what they understand and produce and what other children understand and produce.

Suggestions. These children are at an age where you, as a parent, can talk about the above concerns and fears, even though the child does not bring them up. Talking about school in general and bringing these topics into the conversation without focusing on any particular concern should help in relieving any stress.

Third Grade. At this grade level, children fear disapproval from their peers and their teacher. They are becoming more competitive; when teams are chosen, they fear that they won't be chosen or will be chosen last. They are beginning to feel more pressure from academic work and demands. They are afraid of taking tests, of getting bad grades, and of not having enough time to complete work. They are also concerned about teachers either calling or writing home and about parent conferences.

Suggestions. Be in frequent communication with the teacher. With your child, explore his or her strengths and weaknesses and help him to understand his limitations. Be very clear about your expectations as a parent. It would also be beneficial to show your child how to organize his or her work.

Fourth Grade. Some of the same fears that are evident in the third grade show up in the fourth: teacher's disapproval, being chosen last for a team or for any activity, and peer disapproval in general. In addition, children at this stage fear not having any friends, being left out, being made fun of, or not being part of a "secret."

Suggestions. Use some of the same suggestions as for a child in grade three. If your child has good social skills, reassure him or her that the same social skills used in making present friends or in dealing with adults will still work. For children who have social difficulties, encourage them to become active in group or team activities. Serious social problems should be addressed professionally.

Fifth Grade. At this level, children fear not passing to the next grade, not measuring up academically, and peer disapproval. Again, they are afraid of being chosen last, of losing their best friend, or of having their friends break a confidence or share a secret.

Suggestions. If your child's grades warrant it, show him or her that retention is not likely to be based on grades. Most schools hesitate to retain a youngster at this level. If retention is likely, however, how you accept it will affect how your child accepts it. Review the suggestions given for grade four.

Sixth Grade. There is an increasing concern about one's sexuality at this level. Cliques are formed; fear of being an outsider is prevalent. Being popular is important; if one is unpopular, any stress is magnified. Social acceptance is emphasized. Children as this level fear not being accepted by teachers, principal, staff, or peers.

Suggestions. Providing information about sexual development and functioning is encouraged. Discuss social skills, expectations, and behaviors.

Junior High School. At this age, children do not want to be singled out, whether chosen first or last. They want to have little attention called to themselves. Their own sexuality continues to be of concern, and they become increasingly aware of their own physical defects, whether imagined or real. They are concerned about their psychological adjustment and their academic success.

Suggestions. As before, provide information about sexual development and functioning. Discuss social skills, expectations, and behaviors. Discuss and reinforce your rules and limits. Provide opportunities for independent experience; increase responsibilities. Listen to the children's concerns about themselves. Remember, any perceived physical blemish is an important issue at this age. Always give praise and encouragement.

Senior High School. At this level, concerns about issues of sexuality are magnified. Adolescents are hesitant about any bodily exposure, they are afraid of failing academically, they are concerned about having enough money, and they are struggling with vocational decisions. Youths at this stage have difficulty in dealing with periods of unhappiness and fear being bored. They also fear confrontations either with authority figures or with peers. They still have concerns with being singled out, whether to lead an activity (and not being sure of themselves) or by being chosen last (and seeing themselves as not desirable). While they are becoming more competitive, they also fear not measuring up. They fear the unknown after graduation, and are afraid of being forced into specific roles by parents or other significant adults. Although they have a desire to be independent, strong dependency needs remain.

Suggestions. Again, refer to previously given suggestions. Remember to keep communication open and to practice your active listening skills. Be available for guidance and help when asked, but don't always force your decisions on adolescents. They need to learn from their own mistakes or experiences (within reason, of course).

What Parents Can Do

Probably it is most important not to make assumptions about what is or is not stressful to your son or daughter. What you may see as stressful may not be at all stressful to your child. The following suggestions will help you and your child or adolescent to understand and cope better with stress.

1. Listen to your children. Sharing worries and concerns helps them to put things in perspective. Here, you can correct any mistaken assumptions about any behavior or event. One of the most important benefits of listening is that it helps children to see that there is a difference between who they are and their behavior.

They will learn that one event doesn't make a good or a bad person.

2. Encourage your children to try some physical activity, which will release the pressure when they are nervous, angry, or upset. Running, walking, or, playing a sport are some of the possibilities. Physical activity will relieve that "uptight" feeling and will relax them. Remember, minds and bodies work together.

3. Help your children to know their limits. If a problem is beyond their control and cannot be changed at the moment, help them to accept what is—at least until they can change it, if that is possible.

4. Teach children to take care of themselves, to get enough rest, to eat well. If they are irritable and tense from lack of sleep or if they are not eating correctly, they will have less ability to deal with stressful situations. If stress continually keeps them from sleeping, ask your doctor for help.

5. Encourage them to make time for fun. There should be time for both work and play. Play can be just as important to their well-being as work; they need a break from their daily routine to relax.

6. Encourage your children to become involved. They won't complain about getting bored, sad, or lonely if they go where (within reason) it's all happening. Sitting alone can make them feel frustrated and more isolated. Encourage them to participate in school and community activities.

7. Suggest that your children make a list of things they have to do. Then have them do these things one at a time and check them off as they are completed. Trying to take care of everything at once can be overwhelming; as a result, nothing may be accomplished.

8. Teach your children cooperation instead of confrontation. Teach them that it's okay to be wrong and that usually there is more than one way of doing things. A little give and take from both sides—parents and

children—will reduce the strain and make everyone more comfortable.

9. A good cry can be a healthy way to relieve anxiety. It might even prevent a headache, stomachache, or other physical symptoms. Tell your children it's OK to cry. Encourage them to take some deep breaths; that can also relieve tension.

10. Reading a good book or playing music can create a sense of peace and tranquility. Some quiet time to dream can be a good escape from tension and frustration.

11. Don't teach your children self-medication. Although drugs can reduce stress temporarily, they do not remove the conditions that caused the stress. Drugs can be habit-forming and can create more stress than they relieve. Think twice before you set an example for your children through your own self-medication. Drugs should be taken only on your doctor's advice.

12. The best strategy for avoiding stress is to learn how to relax and to teach your children how to do so. Remember that you can't relax at the same pace as you lead the rest of your life. Teach your children how to tune out their worries about time and productivity, at least for a while. Encourage them to find satisfaction in just being, without striving, and to find activities that give them pleasure and are good for their mental and physical well-being. From time to time, the focus should be on relaxation, enjoyment, and health.[23]

13. Encourage your children to make friends. Being able to turn to someone, either an adult or a peer, can provide necessary relief, support, or comfort. It is not necessary to have many friends and to be the most popular. What is important is the quality of the relationships.

14. Children and adolescents who react to stress by withdrawing or by overreacting with impulsive behavior would benefit by learning how to become pleasantly assertive. Encourage your children to express their

opinions, needs, and wants in an open, pleasant way. Self-esteem is increased when children or adolescents are confident in their own abilities.

15. Encourage your children to problem solve (see chapter 9). Many young people do not have the slightest idea of what is involved in this process. Teach them to look at alternatives and to try to foresee the consequences of their behaviors.

16. Teach children and adolescents how to identify stress in a variety of situations. In this way they can respond to a stressful event in a more organized, better-thought-out manner.

17. Children and adolescents may be overwhelmed with stressors. If one of these stressors can be removed, canceled, or put aside for a time, their strategies for handling other stressors may increase. Ask your child to list all the stresses that he or she is aware of; then try to resolve one or two of them.

18. Encourage children or adolescents to try different ways of coping with stress: joking, helping others, sports, or social activities, as well as other coping strategies mentioned earlier in this chapter.

Young people often do not receive the time and attention necessary to develop into competent human beings who have a good measure of self-esteem and respect. They feel the stress of being left out, of being second best, or of not being important enough to focus on. Most children and adolescents do not have sufficient inner strength to develop normally without the support and attention of loving parents. In addition, youths subject to stress have been shown to be more prone to both medical illness and injury.

The fact that many children and adolescents are able to cope with stress suggests that stress reduction can be learned if guidance and support are given.

8

Talking, Listening, Communicating

I F we, as practicing psychologists, were to list the most common problems found in families, communication and parenting skills would be among the top items. Serious communication barriers between parents and their children create a stress that could place the children at a high risk for depression, even for suicide. There are many ways in which communication can be blocked or never even established.

Patterns of communication, both verbal and nonverbal, that encourage a child or a teenager to commit suicide are established in suicidal families. Parents might ignore or not listen to their children when they are trying to express their suicidal thoughts. It's not unusual for a parent or a friend to turn and walk away from the child or adolescent upon hearing the first hint of suicidal talk. Sometimes a family member will cut off a person in the middle of a conversation if that conversation begins to focus on suicide. Verbal messages that encourage a person to take his or her own life are not uncommon. In an attempt at reverse psychology, people have been heard to say, "Go ahead. See if I care," when someone says, "I'm going to kill myself." A child's efforts to express his or her feelings of being unhappy, frustrated, or afraid of failing are often not accepted by the parents. All of these patterns intensify any negative feelings that children and adolescents have, and only isolate them further. Often an attempt at suicide is their way of trying to break down communication barriers so that people important to them will know how desperate they feel.[1]

For children who have physically ill parents, neither the parents nor the children will share their problems, as each is attempting to protect the other. Children who have parents with emotional problems usually develop communication skills and patterns that protect them from their parents' negative reactions.[2] Unfortunately, these types of communication skills are not effective and they make survival very difficult.[3]

Another form of negative communication pattern is what is called the "expendable child." This pattern suggests that certain parents have a conscious or unconscious belief that a child is bad or is a burden. If this happens within a family and if this attitude is shown directly or indirectly to the child, the child develops a wish to die. An example of this is seen in our own clinical experience. Richie, the child discussed in chapter 1, was an unwanted five-year-old boy. He was told repeatedly by his mother that he was "a bother" and was the cause for his father's desertion. The mother often said that she "would be happy" if Richie were not around. In his kindergarten class, Richie began to fight with his friends and attempted to cut his arm with a pair of scissors. Frequent accidents occurred; each accident became more serious until Richie finally succeeded in ending his life in a "bike accident."

Barriers to Communication

Communication should be a bridge between people, not a barrier. If good communication habits are not developed when the children are young, the barriers may serve to keep adults at a distance in the adolescent years. Let's look at some of the more typical types of communication barriers.[4]

Differences in Generations

This barrier is used effectively by children, adolescents, and adults. The result is that each generation believes that the other has nothing to offer. Usually very universal statements begin the blocking process, such as the following:

"When I was your age, I didn't have life this easy. I had to get out of school and work. You—you've got your own TV, stereo, new car. What more could you want?"

"My parents don't know a thing about sex."

"What does she know? She's just a baby."

"My folks are so dumb."

Each side has an opinion, but neither side is listening.

Put-Downs or Labeling

Often adults believe that if they can "label" a behavior for a child or an adolescent, the individual will be able to see it and change his or her ways. Once the behavior is identified, many adults feel they have done their job. Unfortunately, what happens is that the adults have managed to put distance between themselves and their child. They have also denied any responsibility for the problem. The child or adolescent is left with feelings of anger and damaged self-esteem because this barrier offers no help in resolving the problem. Here are some examples:

Being Critical or Calling Names

"You're a jerk."
"Why are you always so stupid?"
"You're nothing but a bum and a troublemaker."
"My child wouldn't be that dumb. I must have got the wrong kid at the hospital."
"What are you? Some sort of clown?"
"You've been a troublemaker ever since you've been in this school."
"If you weren't such a brat, your father would have never left."
"You shithead!"
"The only trouble with you. . . ."

These types of comment simply result in guilt feelings, poor self-esteem, and resentment. They could also cause the child to believe what was said to the extent that personality development is negatively influenced.

Having All the Answers

"You're just going through a phase."
"You're just tired."
"You always act that way."
"You're mad at the whole world."
"You're wrong."

These types of comment arouse anger and resentment. The child or adolescent then questions whether he or she is capable and has the ability to deal with life's problems. Such comments really say to the child or adolescent, "I know everything and you know nothing."

Sarcasm—One of the Worst Barriers

"Why don't you leave home while you have all the answers?"
"No one knows anything but you!"
"You're right; the world's wrong."
"You know everything."
"What a dumb thing to say."

These comments build anger and hostility as well as reflect rejection by the adult.

Being constantly ignored, put down, insulted, or ridiculed not only establishes poor self-esteem but also effectively stops a youth from attempting any communication.

In some instances the child or adolescent, if put down or labeled in front of his or her friends, will try to live up to that reputation.

Power Plays

In a power play each side has its own motivations and goals, which are usually unacceptable or are not seen by the other side. The power play is often made up of verbal habits and is used in the following ways:[5]

Ordering

"Don't sit around the house moping all day. Get out and do something."
"Because I want you to do it."
"Because I said so."
"Stop the hysterics; I don't want to hear it."
"You could do it if you really wanted to."

These types of comment tell the child or adolescent that you don't really care about his or her feelings. All these comments do is make the youth want to get even or rebel. They could also influence personality development in a negative direction so that the youth may become shy and withdrawn.

Prescribing

"Your problem is that you're lazy and don't apply yourself."
"If you would only. . . ."
"I told you that you'd make a mess if you did it that way."
"Here, let me do it."
"You don't know what you're doing. It's done like this."

These comments imply that you have little, if any, faith in the child's ability, intelligence, or judgment. It leaves him or her feeling helpless and angry, with little motivation to try new challenges.

Lecturing

"If you had listened to me in the first place, you wouldn't be in this mess."
"There are other fish in the sea."
"Rome wasn't built in a day."
"What you don't realize is. . . ."
"You're too young to understand."

This type of comment simply opens the door for argument. It closes off communication and puts the child or adolescent into an angry, defensive mood.

Giving Advice

"If I were you. . . ."
"This is what you should do."
"Let me tell you what to do."
"I know more about this than you do."

These comments say to children and adolescents, "I'm better than you." It doesn't give them the opportunity to learn for themselves or to feel the pride that results in successful completion of a task or in solving a problem.

Sermonizing

"Nice girls don't; bad girls do."
"You should be ashamed of yourself."
"It's a sin."
"It's the only decent thing to do."

Comments of this type tend to produce guilt and contribute to feelings of poor self-worth. They emphasize what "others" think as a standard that one should live up to.

Withdrawal and Silence

"I don't want to talk about it."
"We'll talk about it later."
"Later."
"That's enough!"
"You've hurt my feelings."

Comments such as these simply raise anxiety in children and adolescents because they don't resolve the issue. Anxiety is often due to indecision; when no decision is made or when issues are left hanging, anxiety lingers. Such comments also reflect a lack of respect for the youth's feelings.

Questioning and Faultfinding

"Whose fault was it?"

"What did you do?"

"Is that the truth?"

"Who did what?"

Faultfinding ignores the child's or adolescent's feelings and emotions; it focuses attention on what happened and on facts. It reflects a lack of trust in the youths, in their behavior, and in their judgment.

In general, a child or adolescent will respond to the above types of comment in a number of ways. These responses range from not listening and tuning them out to momentarily agreeing ("OK, I'll do it in a minute") to angry acting-out behavior such as slamming things around or storming out of the room.

These verbal communication barriers tell the child or adolescent that he or she has no control and that adults are not at all interested in his or her feelings. The breakdown in communication is then complete; neither side is listening to the other. The result is angry feelings and issues that are now harder to resolve.

Social Front

Some parents are thoroughly involved with their status in the community. They see their children as not conforming to their standards of behavior or achievement. These parents may nag, ridicule, or withhold favors, all to no avail. Their children do not listen, and seem to go out of their way to "embarrass" them. Often these children feel as if they are only objects.

Some of these parents feel as if they should have total control over their children. A common theme with this type of parent is that the children should accept the parents' ideas, goals, and values. The children see their parents as being concerned only with what others think about them. These children feel very much alone and are unable to share their own hopes, goals, and dreams with their parents. If the child tries to establish his or her independence, the parent views the child as rebellious and ungrateful; meanwhile the child views the parent as a tyrant and as unapproachable.

"What will the neighbors think if you don't go to college? I want you to go to Yale."

"What do you mean, you want to go to art school? What are you, some kind of fag or something? Just wait till the guys hear about you."

"B is nice, but why didn't you get an A? The _____s' daughter made high honors."

"I don't want you to date Tom. His father's a drunk and Tom's going to be just like him."

In reversed situations, children also become adept at the social front game.

"Mom, you are so out of date. Jane's mom is. . . ."

"Not fair."

"You are so fat, you gross me out."

"You're from another space plane."

The message is clear: the recipient is lacking as a worthwhile person. Why else wouldn't the sender accept them as they are?

Mixed Messages

Saying one thing and meaning another is a very common cause of confusion and blockage. This is an especially important issue to teenagers, who are attempting to become independent and are trying out a new identity. If there are no clear-cut rules or standards for the youth to fall back on, the growing-up process is harder.

A mixed message can sour a success, cause confusion, indicate that a parent is not really proud of the child, sabotage enjoyment, suggest that an achievement wasn't worthwhile, place a youth in a no-win situation, and put a youth down. Mixed messages include the following:

"Yes, you can go cruising, but I'll worry about you the whole time you're gone."

"I was really proud of you when you got up all by yourself to get ready to go, but you made a mess in the kitchen. Why can't you ever remember to turn off the lights?"

"So big deal, you made the second-string football team. What's wrong with you that you didn't make first string?"

"How come, if you're so smart, you didn't make first honors?"

By giving mixed messages, the parent actually may be encouraging an undesirable behavior.

Parents aren't the only ones who give mixed messages. Often a youths mix behavioral, feeling, or verbal clues indicating possible suicidal intent. For instance, they may withdraw from family and friends, show a decline in school performance, increase risk taking, run away, or act out in many ways. They may deny that they have any problems. When asked how they feel about something, they may deny having any feelings or thoughts about it. They may become depressed or sad, and may cry excessively. They may be angry and hostile. They may even make direct statements such as "I feel like killing myself" or indirect statements such as "I can't go on like this." Yet when these youths are confronted with the possibility of suicide, there is strong denial. They will often say, "I was just joking," "I didn't mean what I said," or "I was just having a bad day." It is difficult to deal with any youth who denies such feelings.

In a recent example of such denial an eighth-grade boy was despondent over failing grades. A classmate had alerted police to his friend's suicidal intentions. When the police and the fire department emergency crew arrived at the boy's home, he assured them that he was only joking. A search of the home failed to turn up any weapon; the chief of police later described the boy as "calm. His attitude was good, and there was no indication of self-hysterics." Soon after the authorities left, the boy shot and killed himself with a 12-gauge shotgun.[6]

Mental health workers also run into denial. It is not unusual for children and adolescents who have attempted suicide to deny their action. They may be afraid of their own behaviors or fear that people will think they are crazy. Reaching these children, although difficult, is not impossible; it is important for the mental health professional not to give up. Active listening, working with the family, and working with the youth will often open up communication.

Overreacting or Underreacting

Although not as serious a communication barrier as some of the above, over- or underreaction can stymie communication.

An adult who overreacts can cause the child or adolescent such distress or guilt that he or she will hide a problem so as to not upset the adult. In an effort to show concern, an adult may ask too many questions. For some children and adolescents, this may be a turn-off. The questions, though meant to express concern, might be seen as intrusive or even hostile. It is better to ask only those questions that are important and to establish an open environment for communication. Often asking questions will sidetrack a youth from what he or she really wants to talk about.

The underreacting adult minimizes what a child or adolescent may feel is a major issue, feeling, or problem. Being told "It doesn't matter" or "Don't get so upset" only conveys that the adult does not understand or is not willing to share the youth's feeling or pain. Underreacting adults may also withdraw from the youth by distancing themselves physically. In such cases the adult may make little or no eye contact or may read or work while the child or adolescent is talking to him or her.

It is a sad commentary on family life that we often treat

friends and acquaintances, even strangers, better than we treat family members. We take the time to listen to others; we offer them understanding; we are not openly critical; we go out of our way to help; we strive to make a good impression; and we treat them with courtesy and respect. When we deal with family members, we often act the opposite. We don't have time because there are too many other things to do; we are impatient because we think *our* children should know better; we are critical of their behavior and of them because we often expect more than they are capable of giving; and we often do not respect them or their feelings, attitudes, and behaviors. To illustrate this difference, we often cite the following example:

Your place of employment gives a party. You pay special attention to your appearance; you are talkative and friendly. You try to create a good impression, treating co-workers and guests with courtesy and respect. In another situation, your spouse's family comes over for dinner. You might not pay any special attention to how you are dressed or how the house looks. You may find yourself impatient with some of the visitors; perhaps you are even openly critical. You don't strive to create a good impression; you may not be very understanding; you may even isolate yourself by watching TV or being occupied in other ways.

Anger

Little, if any, positive communication takes place when we are angry and hurt. Our aim is to hurt the other person in return. Instead of listening to that person, we use the time when he or she is talking to think about what we want to say and to make our points. We also use that time to remember past hurts and anger, which we then use to increase our present anger.

An example is a parent who is angry and is disciplining a child for some present misbehavior. Meanwhile the parent remembers past incidents that made him or her angry about the child. The parent uses that past anger to increase the present anger.

Nonverbal Messages

From infancy children can receive nonverbal messages of approval or disapproval. In fact, children and adolescents have an uncanny instinct for picking up the attitudes of the adults around them. Nonverbal messages are given in such a variety of ways that it is difficult always to be aware of them. Such messages are sent by gestures, postures, facial expressions, or a certain tone of voice. A person's posture, a shrug of a shoulder, a lift of an eyebrow, or a voice level can convey a signal to those around. Consider, for example, the mother who does not like her sixteen-year-old daughter's best friend but pretends that she does. The daughter is confused and even angry at times because of her mother's syrupy sweetness toward her friend. Because of these angry, confused feelings, she begins to doubt her mother in other areas: "If my mother is lying about liking my friend, what else does she try to cover up?"

When words say one thing while behavior says another, the mixed message puts the child or the adolescent in a bind; does the adult feel acceptance or nonacceptance? Approval or disapproval? Being placed consistently in such a bind over a long period can be emotionally damaging. Feelings of discomfort and frustration build up when one does not know which behavior to choose because of those mixed messages. In the above example the daughter began to doubt her mother, but many children and adolescents doubt themselves. They rely on their parents and the adults around them to be truthful; when a mixed message is given, it must be they who are "mixed up." The internal mechanism that keeps them on an even keel becomes unbalanced. What is true is false and what is false is presented as true.

Tone of Voice. Children pick up messages from our tone of voice. If our tone matches our words, they receive a consistent message. When tone and words differ, they usually hear the tone of voice. It is through our tone of voice that children often hear our acceptance or our rejection, our pride or our disappointment, our interest or our disinterest, our concern or our lack of concern, our love or our indifference. Our voice can be cold or warm, hard or soft, tender or cruel. The important factor is that our tone of voice and our words match.

Body Language. We give our children messages by the way we stand and carry ourselves. Standing and facing someone with our arms folded across our chest or our hands on our hips is a sign of blame or authority. Turning sideways or with our back to someone implies a lack of interest, as does walking away.

Facial expressions are a very important part of any relationship and of communication. Smiling can express love and acceptance; in the form of a sneer, it can express anger and rejection. Narrowed eyes and tight lips and jaw can express anger.

Unless body language is accompanied by verbal communication on the part of both the giver and the receiver, the true meaning of the message is generally unknown.

Good Communication Patterns

Good communication patterns consist of both listening and talking. It is one thing to feel acceptance toward your child or adolescent; it is quite another to have your child or adolescent feel it. Adults need to show acceptance nonverbally as well as verbally.[7] When your child is involved in an activity that is safe and acceptable and if you don't intrude in that activity, you show acceptance of and confidence in your child. Passive listening—saying nothing but being attentive—conveys the fact that your child is worth listening to.

Nonverbal Acceptance

How do you communicate acceptance nonverbally? Demonstrating affection, nonintervention (not intruding) in an activity, and passive listening are all possible techniques.

Affection. Demonstrating affection, which can increase physical closeness and improve communication between a parent and a child, can be done in many ways. Remember that there are times when a child or an adolescent does not want to be hugged or kissed. You should respect that fact. Therefore the ways of showing affection should be changed. Hugs and kisses express love, but so does touching your child's hair, putting an arm around your child's shoulder for a moment, giving a pat on the back, sharing a treat, or simply sitting together on the sofa. All of these gestures convey warmth; are all ways of saying, "I accept you." Children, adolescents, and adults all need physical affection and acceptance.

Nonintrusion. Nonintrusion into a child's or adolescent's activity may seem at first to contradict the idea of communicating, sharing an interest, and being involved. Nonintrusion, however, means letting children or adolescents work through a problem or complete a project on their own. If a parent always puts in his or her two cents' worth or always takes control, the children never learn that they are competent persons who can take care of themselves. Never letting a person finish a task conveys the message that that person is not competent or able to handle life on his or her own. The mother who remakes a child's bed and the father who always has something to say about how a child does a task show how parents can intrude unknowingly into their child's or teen's life under the guise of "doing it right" or "being helpful." How much better it would be if parents could stand back and could watch and appreciate the satisfaction and self-confidence that their children earn when they complete a task through their own efforts. Keep in mind, however, that a parent must intervene when the child's safety and well-being are at stake.

Eric was excited about being in his first soapbox derby. He was especially pleased with his creation. Unfortunately, his father was also excited and wanted his son "to win." As a result, Eric's father took over and Eric lost all enthusiasm for the project, saying, "It's not mine anymore." The outcome? Eric won the soapbox derby, but at the expense of several feelings. His father was angry at Eric for "sulking" when all he was doing was "helping him win." Eric was angry at his father for taking over, and withdrew emotionally. What messages were given? Eric felt that he wasn't good enough to build his own car. His father felt misunderstood, with a "brat" for a son.

An opportunity was missed here. If Eric's father could have stood back, offered advice when asked, given praise when it was deserved, and let Eric do his own project, the outcome could have been a bond between father and son. Eric might not have won the derby, but the time together, shared in a nonintrusive way, would have won a better memory for the two of them.

Passive Listening. Silence—or passive listening—is used effectively by many mental health professionals. Just by listening and saying nothing—or by saying very little—you can make a person feel accepted. You can encourage a person to talk or to say more by making simple comments such as these:

"Tell me more about it."

"I'd like to hear about it."

"Tell me the whole story."

Active Listening. More successful is active listening, in which the listener tries to understand what the speaker is feeling. The listener, by using his or her own words, then interprets the feelings, along with what has been said. The speaker then can then react to the interpretation.[8] This process allows misunderstandings to be cleared up before feelings are acted upon or repressed. An example of active listening follows:

MOTHER: Would you please do the dishes?

DAUGHTER: I always have to do the dishes!

MOTHER: You're angry at me because I asked you and not your sister.

DAUGHTER: Yes, she never does anything!

Ideally, parents should use normal conversational tones when talking with children. They should give explanations or ask questions in the same tone as when talking with friends. It is important for adults not to speak in one way with children and in another with adults. Asking open-ended questions, which need answers other than a "yes" or a "no," is an excellent way to encourage communication.[9]

The good thing about active listening is that it helps to reduce misunderstanding and misinterpretation as well as cutting down on anger. Active listening can help children to develop self-esteem as well as to understand and express their thoughts better. By using active listening, you can reduce misunderstandings. Your child will feel good because you have obviously listened and have become involved. Active listening will also help you to understand and improve your own communication skills.

In summary, it is possible for serious communication barriers between parents and children to create such high stress that children can be placed at serious risk for depression and even suicide. Good communication is the foundation for positive mental health and emotional growth.

9

Parenting Skills

THIS chapter is not meant to be an in-depth analysis of parenting; rather it focuses on key parenting skills that we have found over the years to be effective with children and adolescents who are depressed and possibly suicidal. For those of you who wish to pursue parenting skills in more depth, several excellent books are available: Dr. Thomas Gordon's *Parent Effectiveness Training, The Parent's Handbook* by D. Dinkmeyer and G.D. McKay, and *How To Discipline without Feeling Guilty* by M.A. Silberman and S.A. Wheelan.[1-3]

Parenting can be highly complex and often totally confusing. Being a parent is the toughest and most important job in the world. That's what it is—a job! A job that requires, among other things, patience, wisdom, diplomacy, and love. Usually a person becomes a parent without any special training, adequate knowledge, or a particular set of skills. Often one's own parents become the model of how a child is to be raised or not raised. In working with teenagers, we commonly hear the statement, "When I have my own kids, I won't treat them like my parents treat me." We seem to find, however, that parents tend to make the same mistakes that their parents made, and that their grandparents made before them. Too often parenting turns out to take a trial-and-error approach, or, at the other extreme, an analytical approach that focuses on every detail of a spoken word or gesture. The analytical approach is especially evident if a child or teenager has made suicidal threats, or (even more dangerous) an attempt. Parents don't know which way to turn. They feel confusion, inadequacy, betrayal, guilt, and anger, seemingly all at once. There is a constant walking on eggshells that affects the whole family.

While parenting is often using one's common sense, it is not reasonable to expect parents to have instant knowledge and acquired skills for loving and caring for a child from infancy to adulthood, especially if that child is depressed and/or suicidal. That's why parenting is a learned skill. In spite of the saying, "You can't teach an old dog new tricks," improved parenting skills, openness to change, and, more important, incorporating those changes into the family can be learned and increased over the years.

Key components to parenting are helping the child develop positive feelings about himself or herself, setting limits and being consistent with those limits, encouraging independence, and accepting the child as he or she is.

Positive Feelings

Positive feelings can be fostered in two ways: by self-esteem and by dependability. Children need positive self-esteem, and this comes from feeling lovable and capable. Children also need to know that there is some important person in their life who is dependable. Conveying these two important messages to your child leaves the child feeling that he or she is a valuable person who deserves to be loved.

Too often, as parents and as adults, we focus on a youth's misbehavior, on what needs to be improved, or on what's not · right about her or him. It's not that we don't see the good and positive side of the youth; rather we tend to overlook or take for granted the youth's strengths and positive qualities.

Consider, for example, a father or a mother talking on the telephone with a friend or a business acquaintance. The child misbehaves, is noisy, or is disruptive. The parent may excuse himself or herself, put down the telephone, and discipline the child. If that child sits quietly and behave, usually the parents says nothing because this type of behavior is expected. But what better way to reinforce the positive behavior than to tell your child how much you liked that behavior?

Techniques for Building Self-Esteem

"I" versus "You" Statements. When a parent makes statements that begin with "I" instead of "You," that parent is better able to give a message about his or her own feelings, needs, and intentions. When a "you" statement is made, the child receives a message of blame and implied criticism. As a result the child becomes defensive and eventually "parent deaf." When an "I" statement is made, there is clarity about what that parent expects and feels. This clarity helps the child feel secure and able to depend upon a parent. The parent is being up front with the child.

An "I" statement has three parts: description, feeling, and consequence.[4] The two necessary parts are the description and the consequence of a behavior; the feeling part is not always necessary.

The first part describes the behavior that is of concern—describes, not blames:

"When I don't get a call telling me that you are going to be late getting home from school . . ."

The second part conveys the feeling about the consequence of that behavior:

"I get worried that something happened to you . . ."

The third part conveys the consequence of the behavior:

"because I don't know where you are."

Compare that statement to the following:

"Why didn't you call me when you knew you were going to be late (accusatory)? You never think about anyone or anything but yourself (criticizing). You could be dead in the street and I'd be the last to know (guilt-provoking)."

These three parts of the "I" statement—description of the

behavior, statement of your feeling, and statement of the consequence—don't have to be in any particular order; nor does the feeling statement always have to be included.

The "I" statement expresses how the parent feels about a situation without promoting blame, guilt, or accusatory opinions. It opens communication.

Appreciation. A technique that's useful in building self-esteem is to take the time with the child to "appreciate." To appreciate a child means to look for the good qualities in that child. Appreciation can be general, such as "I'm glad I'm your mother," or specific, such as "I liked the way you played with your sister."

Giving a child a sense of his or her history is another way to show appreciation. This process also helps the child to relate good qualities from the past to the present. All children like to hear stories of things they did when they were little; they often don't remember their past. To be told of the good things that they did helps in building their self-esteem: for instance, "When you were just five years old you were the fastest runner around" or "I remember one day when it was raining and I was really sick, you made me lunch."

Also remember to turn appreciation around. This step teaches the skills to the child. Ask children to relate what they like about a sibling, a friend, a pet, a parent, a relative, or themselves. For example, encourage the child to think, "What's the best thing about going to Grandma's house?" or "What the very best thing about you?"

When parents take the time to appreciate their children and then to encourage the children to learn how to use this skill for themselves, the children feel good about themselves.

Special Time. Every day for five or ten minutes, or once a week, or whenever possible, set aside a special time to be spent alone with each of your children. In these hurry-up-and-wait times there seems to be less time for our family and for ourselves, so the special time spent with a child is even more important. Time together could mean taking a walk, going to the library, having breakfast or lunch together, reading a book, making cookies, or just playing a game. Special time is not always a long period, but rather a time to be close. It is a sharing time when a parent focuses positive attention on the child, a time that's spent talking to that child about him or her, and not about brothers or sisters. The special time is meant to be enjoyable, not to be spent lecturing, correcting, or pointing out faults. Listening to the child creates a sense of importance and self-worth in that child.

"Let's be Good to _____" Day. While the special time doesn't have to be a whole day, a day that is set aside for a special treat or for a series of little treats is like declaring a holiday for that child. There's Mother's Day, Father's Day, Labor Day, and Memorial Day, so why can't there be a special day for your child, a "Let's be good to _____" day? Again, the idea is to give positive attention to that child, special time for a special person. The message is "I must be someone special to have a holiday all my own."

During or even after a special time, let the child know that you enjoyed that time. Comments such as "It's fun swinging with you. You can swing so high, higher than even I can swing," or "I really enjoyed having breakfast with you today," convey the message that the child is enjoyable and create a tie between parent and child.

Nicknames. Give a positive nickname to the child. Families often have pet names for children; a positive nickname that a child can be proud of increases that child's positive feelings about himself or herself. Even though parents don't realize it, a nickname labels a child. Names such as "Family Fool," "Shithead," "Clumsy," "Stupid," or any other negative name give those messages to the child. The parents may argue that they are only joking, that the child doesn't really take it seriously, or that it's said lovingly. That doesn't matter. It is still negative labeling. How does the child perceive that nickname? All too often he or she internalizes the label. After all, who, in the child's eyes, knows that child best? His or her parents. Therefore, "If mom and dad think of me as a jerk, then that's what I really must be, a jerk."

It's just as easy to give a positive nickname as a negative one. "Tony Terrific," "Princess," "Handsome," "Doll Face," and "Super Guy" all describe something positive about a child. It is much better to have a child internalize a positive than a negative label.

Labeling an action, attribute, or trait is another form of internalizing a belief. Saying to a child as he spills the milk that he is clumsy and pointing out his clumsiness to him every time he trips or bumps into something only accents the negative. Instead of criticizing a child for being clumsy, guide and give suggestions instead. You could suggest, "Be careful and carry the glass with both hands." Guidance, if the child is uncoordinated, might include getting him or her involved in sports, swimming, dance, or gymnastics.[5]

We often see an attribute or a trait in one specific situation, and then, whether it's correct or not, carry that label over into other areas. For instance, the child who is shy may be shy only around adults. Around friends, he or she may chat and play quite happily with others. Stating to other adults that your child will talk when he or she is comfortable implies that the child is able to take part in the conversation. The message to the child is that you understand and have confidence in his or her ability to handle the situation.

Setting Limits

All children need and want limits. They want to know how far they can go in their demands, and that their world is safe. They want to know that someone is in control of their world, someone they can depend on. They want to know they are loved because someone cares and watches out for them. It is a disservice to children not to set limits. It is even a greater disservice when the parents set limits and then do not adhere to them. This situation confuses the child; the significant people in his or her world convey conflicting messages, demands, expectations, and consequences. Most important of all, the child does not develop a secure feel for the world around. When parents do not set limits and adhere to them, the child internalizes feelings of not being important enough or worth the effort for the love, guidance, and discipline that are required in setting those limits. The child may develop feelings that if the parents don't care, why should the child? In addition, the child learns that rules don't have to be followed.

Parents do care but don't always have the emotional and physical energies to keep the rules. They are not always able to see the gray areas where adjustment or bending of the rules is needed. All too often in our practice, we see parents who have an inconsistent parenting style: one parent is lenient or too soft, while the other is strict or too hard. Usually each parent views himself or herself as compensating for the other parent's soft or hard tendencies.

Frequently the "too-soft" parent will try to act as a buffer zone between a youth and the "too-hard" parent. Several problems can arise from this strategy.

1. An alliance is formed between the lenient parent (whom the child perceives as the "good guy") and the child. This alliance works to keep the strict (or "bad") parent out of the picture, and in effect weakens the parental unit.

2. The child very quickly learns how to manipulate both parents. Thus he or she gains the control in the family.

3. The credibility of both parents is lessened. The message is given to the youth that neither parent knows what he or she is doing.

4. When one parent negates the actions of the other, there is a reaction. The parent who has been circumvented may throw up his or her hands and withdraw from the situation or come on even harder than before. As a result both parents become angry ("That's just like him. He leaves everything for me to handle.") and/or hurt ("I don't have any say in this house. All they want from me is to keep the house clean/bring home the paycheck").

It is not necessary that parents have either a lenient or a

strict style. Each family is different; the style that works or is comfortable for one family may not be right for another. What is necessary is consistency. Keep the messages clear and direct, don't change the rules in the middle of a game, and follow through with stated consequences or rewards.

Techniques for Setting Limits

Develop clear rules. Communication is an essential part of establishing rules and an important aspect of parenting—so important that an entire chapter of this book, "Communication," has been devoted to it. When setting limits with your child, keep the message simple, short, and to the point, giving a reason for the rule and stating the consequences or rewards for actions. "Susan, I want you home by nine o'clock because it's a school night. You can stay out later Friday night." Remember the KISS rule: "*K*eep *I*t *S*imple, *S*tupid."

Use language that is appropriate for the child's age and developmental level. Do not use vague words and comments. State the request clearly in language that is understood.

Eliminate vagueness. When vague statements are made, the recipient is left up in the air and the way is open for nagging or a confrontation. We run into trouble in giving clear messages when we aren't sure of our feelings about something. We don't know whether or not we should take a stand on a particular issue, or we have an uneasy feeling about a situation but don't know why. In both of these situations there are ways to lessen vagueness.

One way is to anticipate the options. Be prepared. Recognize that there will be times and situations where you aren't sure what your actions should be. In these cases it is extremely helpful to fall back on thought-out choices. That's why it's necessary to try to anticipate what choices can be made. Choice Number One: go along. Two: ignore and do nothing about the situation. Three: list possible alternatives. Four: take a stand. For example, consider a situation where your son or daughter wants to get a bizarre haircut. Do you respect your child's need to develop his or her own identity, or is it even an identity issue? Do you want the child to conform to your social standards, or is it all right to express himself? The basic issue is that you don't know whether or not you should permit the haircut. Your choices are as follows:

1. Go along; it will grow back eventually.
2. Ignore the request and hope that the child will forget about the idea. This probably won't happen. Ignoring a request in effect gives tacit approval to the plan.
3. Try to compromise by suggesting modifications to the haircut: "No, you can't shave your head, but you can have it cut as short as you want."
4. Say "No" or "It's your decision." Having a mental road map of alternatives at least gives you a focus in decision making.

The second way to eliminate vagueness is to be up front and say, "I don't know." This is not being vague; it's a direct statement. Vague statements such as "We'll see," "I'll think about it," or "Mmmmm," only leave a person hanging in the air. A direct "I don't know," followed by an expression of your feelings and a statement that you're going to think about it for a specified amount of time, is a clear message. "I don't know if I want you to go to that party because I feel uneasy about letting you go to someone's house who I don't know. Let me talk it over with Dad and I'll let you know by this afternoon so that you can make your plans one way or the other."

Clear messages express a person's needs, wants, desires, and expectations.

Be direct. Don't hide a request in the form of a question; this approach indicates that you're unsure of yourself and of how you feel. By making a statement instead of asking a question, you may lessen resistance.

Consider the question, "Susan, do you want to clean your room now?" Because the last thing Susan wants to do is to clean her room, her response would probably be "not now" or "later." It would have been much better to say, "Susan, clean your room." True, Susan still might respond with "later," but your message is direct and Susan's opportunities for manipulation are lessened.

Develop a joint language. Try developing a common language between yourself and your child by teaching and sharing key words, phrases, or expressions. Teach words that are used to describe people's actions and feelings, such as *left out, lost, confident, threatening, acceptance, able, tense, stressed,* and *upset.* Teach phrases or pet expressions that can be a nonthreatening or a humorous signal for a complex communication.[6]

Involve the family in making up these shorthand expressions, such as the following:

"I draw the line" means "That's it, I've had enough, no more pushing the limits."

"The gremlins are at it again" acknowledges mischief but sidesteps a confrontation.

"Up, up, and away" means that it's best to clear out and leave someone alone for a while.

Rules

Reasonability and enforceability. Rules should be reasonable and within the child's ability and developmental level. Rules also need to be enforceable. You need to think the rules through carefully because they are long-term decisions regulating your child's movement, belongings, responsibilities, relationships, and living habits.[7] Here are examples of the various types of rules:

A rule concerning a child's movement could be "Stay in the yard" or "Be home by eleven o'clock."

A belongings rule might be "Don't leave your bike in the drive" or "No one else is to drive your car."

Rules for responsibilities are statements such as "Do your homework before you go out to play" or "Set the table for dinner."

Examples of relationship rules are "Don't hit your brother" or "Stay out of your sister's tape collection."

Living habit rules could be "No eating between meals" or "Take a shower."

Rules are necessary for children. They create feelings of competence, security, responsibility, and the ability to control their own actions and impulses.

Involvement. Although no one likes rules or regulations, they are a necessary part of life. When establishing rules, discuss and explain them with your child because children don't always see the necessity for a rule. Providing opportunities for discussing and explaining rules permits them to express ideas and thoughts about how this rule will affect them. They may have ideas for improving a rule so that it is agreeable and workable for them. In this way you are ensuring that your child understands and holds some responsibility for the process. The rules will be more enforceable and there will be less resistance if your child feels that he or she has some control.

Negotiation. At times, rules are laid down that are neither reasonable nor enforceable. When this occurs, parents sometimes feel that if they give in, they suffer a defeat. They feel that they will have lost face and that their authority will be undermined. They have constant confrontations with the child to try to enforce the rule. This situation leaves both sides deadlocked in a struggle that neither can win, and increases resistance to rules in other areas. In these situations it is best to negotiate because both sides are involved in a no-win situation.

Negotiation does not signal defeat for the parents; it can strengthen the communication and emphaty between the two sides. Negotiation can take many forms and options and can be as creative as both parties involved.

The Smiths were an active family; both parents worked and the children were heavily involved in school and various sports activities. Mr. and Mrs. Smith were both high achievers with high expectations for their children, Mark and Carol. After-school responsibilities for the children were emptying the dishwasher, setting the table, helping with food preparation, and beginning at least some of their homework before dinner.

Carol was a freshman in a private high school, with heavy demands to be on the honor roll and to play softball. She always had softball practice after school in addition to several hours of homework. By the time she came home from practice, she was so tired, rushed, and frustrated that she couldn't accomplish everything and still have time for herself. Her parents, both with heavy career demands, felt equally tired, rushed, and frustrated. They felt that the children needed to be responsible because they, as parents, also needed time for themselves. Because Carol couldn't handle everything that she had to do, Mark had to do more. Mark was angry because he was being asked to do more of Carol's jobs.

Both children felt that their parents were being unfair. The more the parents demanded, the less the jobs were completed, and the confrontations increased. The Smiths did not want to back down from their positions. They felt that the children needed to keep to their commitments. As time progressed and there was no resolution to the conflicts, other jobs were affected.

In reality, what occurred was a stalemate. The Smiths, however, could change from a stance of trying to be in control to one of negotiation. A family discussion was held in which each person stated his or her feelings and then responded to the problem at hand. Although the end results were compromises, the underlying feelings were that everyone felt they had been understood by the others; the children had a say in how responsibilities were to be handled; more important, everyone felt a commitment to working out the problem. On nights when there was softball practice, Carol was excused from her chores, but she assumed extra jobs on the weekend. Both Mark and his parents took the extra evening chores.

Additional ways to negotiate are as follows:

Give choices about how, when, and where. For example,

instead of demanding that the grass be mowed Saturday morning let the child decide on a good time (within reason, of course). Perhaps there is a game that the child wants to attend, so the afternoon would be less hurried for him or her. As long as the grass is mowed on the weekend, does it really matter exactly when it is done? As in everything, there are exceptions; the reasons for these exceptions should be explained. "The grass needs to be mowed this morning because the company will be here at any time. I want everything finished and you cleaned up."

Offer alternatives. When a request is not possible and the adult's answer is "no," provide alternatives to satisfy the needs of the person making the request. For example, a child wants to go fishing with his father, but the father has too much work to do that day, or perhaps doesn't feel up to it. The father can sympathize with his son's desire to go fishing, but because it's not possible, perhaps they can play ball together instead.

Exchange one responsibility for another. As seen in the previous example, Carol was able to exchange her afternoon responsibilities for different ones on Saturday.

Compromise. When neither side can have all of its needs met, a compromise is a good solution. Carol felt that her responsibilities were too great at that particular time. A compromise was reached whereby her parents and her brother took on some of her jobs until the end of her softball season.

Have the child suggest a solution. Just because you're an adult doesn't mean you have all the answers. Sometimes the child can come up with a good solution. For example, Tom is unhappy because he has to walk the dog. He suggested that he be allowed to walk the dog down the street to a friend's house. He could walk the dog, still be able to see his friend, and be home by supper time.

Hold a family meeting to reach a solution together. The best way to solve the problem is to brainstorm. When there is a conflict, write down as many alternatives as possible, realizing that what is written is not binding, but only a list of ideas. Then discuss which idea might work for both the adult and the child. For instance, Sally and her mother were in conflict over Sally's tying up the phone. The solution was for Sally to try to use the phone during a certain time period.

Assumptions. One of the difficulties that parents fall into is assuming that just because they've said something a hundred or even a thousand times, the child will understand. Be specific; tell children exactly what is expected or wanted from them. Does "Clean up your room" mean to get everything out of sight, toys under the bed, clothes thrown in the closet, bedspread pulled up over the pillows? That may be how the child understands "Clean up your room." An adult's understanding is different, but he or she assumes that the child knows that dirty clothes go in the hamper, clean clothes are folded and put in drawers or hung in the closet, and toys are put in a box. It is much easier to start out by being specific. "I want you to clean your room. Remember to put the dirty clothes in the hamper." It's OK, even necessary, to keep repeating and to sound like a broken record.

You have more impact when you use specific language ("Put your dirty clothes in the hamper") rather than general language ("Clean your room").

There is an additional advantage to using specific language. Some children see a responsibility as overwhelming or never-ending. When specific instructions are given one at a time, the child develops the feeling that he or she can manage.

Never assume that the rules are clear. Work out the small details together with the child.

Consequences. In rule making, the consequences, either positive or negative, should be thought out ahead of time. When a rule is not followed, the adult should have an idea of the consequence, keeping in mind that different infractions require different kinds of consequences. All too often, if the adult has not thought of a consequence, either an overreaction, with an unenforceable punishment, or an underreaction, with no punishment, could occur. "You're grounded for a month" might sound good when you're frustrated and angry, but is it enforceable or fair? Remember that the parent has the responsibility to follow through with the punishment. Not following through with a stated consequence only confirms to the child that rules don't have to be followed.

Modeling. Expect your child to model your behavior. The parent should be a positive role model for the child. If you have a rule that the child is to call home when he or she will be late for dinner, it is helpful if the child sees that the parents also call if they are delayed.

Consistency and Resistance

Trying to be consistent and to follow through with the consequences is probably more difficult for the adults than following the rules is for the children. There may be times when children comply readily. Then, for no apparent reason and no matter what the adult does, there is noncompliance or resistance. Power struggles are to be avoided because both sides are losers, but how does an adult get the child to follow the rules? There are many effective ways to handle resistance.

First, you need to investigate whether special circumstances are preventing a child from complying. In the example of Carol and Mark, both children felt that at that particular time the rules were unfair. To indicate their unhappiness and resentment, they showed a resistance that carried over to other job areas. The Smiths' solution was to negotiate and compromise. They accomplished this at a family meeting where everyone had a chance to voice an opinion.

Second, children who are depressed may be emotionally unable to "pull it together." Their emotional energy is being used in other areas and there is nothing left. Often, to be held responsible is one more stress that can not be handled. These children have a need for the adult to be sensitive and open to compromise.

Third, understand that it is the child who must be responsible for a behavior. Expecting that the child will follow the rules, with or without the presence of an authority figure, puts that child in charge of his or her behavior.

Techniques for Avoiding Resistance

Broken Record. The broken record technique is used only when the adult is sure of his or her position, when there will be no compromise, when the adult knows what he or she wants, or when the child is not giving an appropriate response. This technique is designed to help make a point and then to stick to it. State your request or refusal repeatedly in a calm, firm voice. Face the child and keep good eye contact. If you meet refusal, don't raise your voice. It is even more beneficial if you can lower your voice somewhat.

The broken record technique works best when the adult is refusing a request rather than trying to get the child to do something.[8] When you need to have the child comply, be prepared for a course of action if he or she refuses. Your action, of course, depends on the child's age and developmental level. In the case of the younger child who refuses to go to his or her room, you should pick up and carry the child. For the teenager who refuses to go to his or her room, you have no choice but to make the consequence more powerful. "Since you won't go to your room, the radio and stereo will be removed for one week." In some cases, it might be more strategic to back off from the request and say firmly, "I had hoped that you would mow the yard. I'll ask you again tomorrow." By backing down from the request, you avoid a power struggle. You will, however, need to repeat the request at the stated time.

Leaving notes to remind the child of a responsibility is a nonverbal broken record. This technique is particularly effective with seven- to twelve-year-old children.

Accentuating the Positive. Accentuate the positive behavior and ignore the bad. This is the favorite technique of psychologists and others in the mental health field. Do not use this method, however, if there is a dangerous situation or a situation where an immediate action or intervention from the adult is required.

To use this technique, you need to be consistent. It won't work if the behavior is sometimes ignored and sometimes responded to. In fact, when there is inconsistency in ignoring the behavior, that behavior will become stronger. Also, it is important to realize that even if you show consistency in ignoring, behavior, it might get worse before it stops. It's almost as if the child says to himself or herself, "I'll put everything I've got into this last try."

The child is trying to get the adult's attention in any way possible. The child who needs attention will accept negative, punitive attention rather than no attention at all. Give this child attention when he or she is not looking for it and when it is not expected.

Rewards. Giving rewards is a time-honored tradition that works. Attaching a reward to a responsibility often entices a child into cooperation. Some parents feel that giving a reward results in manipulation by the child, but in reality, there is a large difference between a reward and a bribe. Manipulation occurs only when a bribe is offered.

For example, a student we saw recently was having difficulty with academic work. In a conference with us and with his parents he stated that he couldn't concentrate on his studies because all he could think about was the new Camaro in the auto dealer's window. He assured his parents that if they bought him the car his studies would improve and he would pass all his subjects. We advised the parents that if they were inclined to buy the car, they should do so only after he passed his courses. We felt that he should be held responsible for his academics without the reward. Against our advice, they did purchase the car. Their son's grades, of course, did not improve; in fact, they got worse and he ended up dropping out of school.

Basically, there are two kinds of rewards: the material and the social. Material rewards include treats, such as money, candy, or toys, or privileges, such as extra curfew time on a weekend, use of the car, or staying overnight at a friend's house. Social rewards include special time spent with a parent, hugs, praise, or any positive strokes.

Material and privilege rewards work only up to a certain point and should not be used consistently. We feel that it's fine to reward occasionally, but only for specific goals. Such rewards quickly reach a saturation point in the child and only lead to bigger demands, with a "what's in it for me?" attitude. Often the child feels that his or her self-worth is directly related to the reward. If the reward is not as expected or is not given, that child might feel that he or she is rejected and is not good enough. Material and privilege rewards work best for activities that are anxiety-provoking, difficult, or unappealing.[9]

It is much better for a child to be inner-directed and responsible. Giving social rewards promotes self-esteem, provides positive communication, develops competency and self-discipline, and spares the family pocketbook.

Silence. Silence is an extremely effective tool and one that parents often don't realize they have. Silence is best used in those situations where the child knows what is expected of him or her. The parent simply observes and waits near the child until the child complies.

In an effective use of silence the child is expected to follow through when a parent makes a request, regardless of excuses or arguments. The parent does not respond to the excuses or arguments.

Recording. A technique that requires a little more work than silence but is also effective is to record over a short period of time the child's behaviors that are of concern. Then review this record with the child, but avoid the shotgun approach; choose only one or two behaviors to record. By having a record of the behaviors, the child is informed that the adult is taking note of him or her and that there is concrete evidence of the behaviors.

After you show the record to the child, inform him or her that you will keep a new record of those specific behaviors for a week. Tell the child that you expect the specific behaviors to be fewer in the coming week; no punishments or rewards will be given. At the end of the week, you and the child will check to see whether there has been a decrease in that particular behavior.

Reverse Psychology. At times, children dig in their heels and prepare to do battle for something. Reverse psychology disarms the child and removes the adult from the battle. This technique, however, is tricky and should be used only in relatively minor situations. In such situations the child chooses to proceed with a behavior in which there is little danger or in which you have an "out." When reverse psychology is used, control is given back to the child. This technique is a valuable learning experience because it allows the child to choose an alternative behavior. Good-natured humor, when combined with this technique, will often provide a format for open communication. Just remember: it's humor, not sarcasm.

In a rather typical example, parents can't stand their son's or daughter's friend. Saying "You can't go out with him (or her)" makes that person seem more desirable. If you forbid the child to have anything to do with the friend, he or she might lie and begin to slip out to see that person. If you do not forbid the child to see the friend, there is a chance that the child will become less attracted to him or her over time.

Refocusing. Refocusing is particularly effective with younger children. It also works on occasion with adolescents, in a much more subtle way. With this method, the child is diverted from one behavior to another. The new behavior should be as interesting to the child as the old. An example of refocusing is the child who is watching TV on a beautiful day when he or she should be outside playing. Offering to bike, swim, or walk with him or her may get the child outside. You may also encourage the child to join others outside who are playing.

Contracts. This is an agreement between adult and child to outline specifically what is expected of each person. It also spells out the consequences, either good or bad, of completion or incompletion. Use the contract only for major behaviors and/or responsibilities. Emphasize only a few issues.

Criticism and Punishment. At times it may be difficult, or perhaps even in appropriate, for a parent to make a positive comment about something that was done poorly. You need to separate work that was attempted but that falls short of your standards or expectations from work that was done without effort or caring. A child who makes his bed but can't tuck in the corners as his mother does needs recognition and praise for his or her efforts. Ripping the bed apart and remaking it is not needed. The child who does his or her homework sloppily needs to know that this behavior is unacceptable. Criticism should be given, but never to tear down a person.

Criticism is necessary and constructive when given in the right way. It should include suggestions on how to do better, or have the child think of a better way himself or herself. If we use the sloppy homework paper as an example, the parent could make a direct statement that the paper is not acceptable, followed by the suggestion that if the child folded the paper or used a ruler to line up the math problems, it would look neater. If the child rushed through the homework, again make a direct statement. Then the child must do the homework over again.

To be effective, punishment should be swift, and hard enough to be impressive. Removal of pleasurable activities or privileges, time-outs, and physical restraint to stop an out-of-control child or a dangerous behavior are all methods of punishment.

Of the punishments listed above, time-outs usually work the best. They do not have to be long; about three minutes is right for the younger child, and perhaps an evening for the older child. The time-outs should be boring, and should be used for only one specific behavior at a time. It's incredible that so many parents use time-outs ineffectively. They send the child to a room that is filled with entertainment—TV, stereo, books, and phone—and then wonder why the punishment is not working.

Figuring Out Their Own Punishment. Make the child responsible for his or her own punishment in situations that are not serious.

Independence

Independence is learned by knowing that one can handle and solve problems. This knowledge creates someone who is competent and self-reliant. The way to promote independence is by providing children with choices and by teaching them to be self-reliant and able to solve their problems.

Techniques for Fostering Independence

Providing Choices. Children will continue to remain dependent on the adults in their world as long as those adults continue to "do" for them. Many parents feel that they are "good" parents because they are involved with their children and do everything for them. In reality, however, these parents are open to manipulation and become doormats for their children's every desire and whim. "Good" parents take the lunch to school when it is forgotten; they drive the child to school so that the child won't have to ride the school bus; if the child doesn't like what's fixed for dinner, they cook a new meal; they hover continuously, reminding the child to button his or her coat, not to forget the sneakers, and so on. They feel responsible for the child's every move, word, and breath.

There are well-intended motives for being a "good" parent. These parents want their child to be happy, never angry; they want him or her to have all the advantages they never had; they want the child to "turn out right"; and they feel that the way the child behaves reflects on them as parents.

By being a "good" parent, one never gives the child the

opportunity to think for himself or herself, to realize fully the limits of the world, or to become a confident and independent person. These children are cheated of life.

Children need to be allowed to make choices and to learn from the consequences of their choices. The best way to learn is to experience; of course, dangerous situations are exceptions.

Problem Solving. In our practice, a great part of our work is teaching children to think through a problem to its conclusion, to try to anticipate the results of a decision, to check out and be prepared to accept the consequences of a choice, and to feel good about themselves even if the choice was wrong. Within the home, parents can instill this skill easily by being the model for the child and by guiding the child through solving a problem on his or her own.

The five steps to problem solving are simple to learn.

1. Know what the problem is. "What's the problem?"
2. Be sure to look at all the alternatives; be creative with them. "What are the choices?"
3. Concentrate and try to anticipate the consequences of a choice. "Think hard."
4. Select a response. "Make a choice."
5. Analyze the choice. If the choice was the right one, be sure that the child learns to give himself or herself a pat on the back. Encourage comments such as "I did great" or "Way to go." If the choice was wrong, encourage the child to consider what would have been a better one. Most important of all, encourage the pat on the back anyway—"I goofed. Well, I'll do better next time"—or a slogan of some type—"That's the way the cookie crumbles. I can handle those crumbs."

Acceptance

Acceptance is conveyed to the child both verbally and non-verbally. Recognizing the child's developmental level can guide a parent in accepting what he or she is able to do. At times more is expected from the child than the child can do or handle, both physically and emotionally. When we communicate to children that we value and respect them, they will respond in a similar fashion and will put forth their best efforts.

Techniques for Acceptance

Active Listening. This technique cannot be stressed enough, and is covered in greater detail in chapter 8. Often parents think they are listening, but in reality they are either parroting or paraphrasing what they have heard. Parroting, or simply repeating the child's words, often makes the child feel as if he or she is being mimicked or even put down. Paraphrasing occurs when the listener uses his or her own words to sum up what has just been said. The difficulty with paraphrasing is that the body language, the intensity, and the tonal quality are ignored.[10] Active listening, if done properly, is difficult. All too often, words are heard but are not listened to.

Active listening is a repeating of both the verbal and the nonverbal messages. Remember, it's not what you say but how you say it that's important. People respond to communication more by how it is given than by words. It's estimated that nonverbal behavior (facial expression) accounts for 55 percent of the communication process, the vocal aspect (tone and volume quality) for 38 percent, and what we say (words) for the remaining 7 percent.[11]

To illustrate the differences among parroting, paraphrasing, and active listening, we give the following examples:

Parroting. Child walks into room and slams down her books.

> CHILD: Allan is so stupid. I hate him. I don't ever want to see him again.
> FATHER: So you think Allan is stupid and you hate him and you don't want to see him again.

Paraphrasing. Child walks into room and slams down her books.

> CHILD: Allan is so stupid. I hate him. I don't ever want to see him again.
>
> FATHER: You're never going to see him again, and he's stupid and you hate him.

Active Listening. Child walks into room and slams down her books.

> CHILD: Allan is so stupid. I hate him. I don't ever want to see him again.

Father notes the slamming of the books and the tears in his daughter's eyes.

> FATHER: I see that you're really upset, angry, and hurt about Allan.

Listening. A good exercise to improve listening skills is to listen to your child for two to five minutes, making an effort not to interpret, become defensive, or angry while he or she is talking. At the end of the time repeat back as much as possible of what the child said, using the child's words. The child then indicates whether you got it right or left something out. Then switch and let the child listen while you talk.

Active Interest. Parents may believe that they are showing an active interest in their child's life by asking questions, but their child may perceive it as snooping. Although it's never too late to show an interest in what's happening in the child's world, it certainly is easier if the parent is actively involved early on. Parents may go wrong in trying to demonstrate an active interest when they fall into the role of policeman. That role uses probing questions. (Remember that there is a definite time and place for probing questions. Such questions as "Where are you going?," "Who's going to be in the car, or driving?," and "Will the parents be home to chaperone the party?" all need to be asked.) Probing questions are not to be used, however, in an attempt to develop closeness and acceptance. When probing questions are asked at an inappropriate time, the child, especially the teenager who values privacy, may react by withholding or omitting information. He or she may attempt to shut the parent out.

The following examples contrast active interest with probing.

Mary comes in from her date and is obviously upset. She is met at the door by her mother, who offers a barrage of questions.

> MOTHER: What's the matter? What happened? Did you two have a fight? Are you OK? Why are you so upset? What did he do?
>
> MARY: Nothing happened. I'm OK.
>
> MOTHER: Where did you go and what did you do? Why are you so upset?
>
> MARY: I'm OK. Nothing happened.

This is an example of a dead-end conversation.

An "active interest" conversation goes as follows: Mary comes in from her date and is obviously upset. She is met at the door by her mother, who says, "Hi, Mary. Gee, hon, it doesn't look like you had a good time at the party."

> MARY: Oh, it was OK.
>
> MOTHER: Could have been a little more fun, huh?
>
> MARY: I'll say. David was a real jerk. He acted like I wasn't even there all night.
>
> MOTHER: It's no fun being ignored.
>
> MARY: I'll say. All the other guys seem to pay attention to me.
>
> MOTHER: Sounds like everyone but the one important to you.

This example gives you a general idea of how you might approach a conversation without a barrage of questions.

Parenting is a difficult task, especially with children who are depressed and possibly suicidal. Part of this difficulty may be due to the parents' fear of making matters worse. Yet how much worse can they get? By not addressing the issues and by not opening up communication, you aggravate the situation. You reinforce the feeling that the child isn't important. In addition to needing structure and limits, children and adolescents need to know that someone not only cares and loves them but really listens to them.

10

Intervention: What to Do When . . .

T WO years previously, Alex's mother had killed herself by
tying a plastic bag over her head. Alex and his older
sister were never told the circumstances of their mother's
death, only that she had died suddenly at home from heart
failure. Alex appeared to have recovered from the shock of
his mother's death and seemed to have adjusted well. His
father and relatives describe him as a typical twelve-year-
old boy, active in Little League and the Boy Scouts.

In the past several months, Alex's mood had changed. His
best friend, Rob, noticed it first. Alex, usually a laid-back
type, became very irritable and overcritical of Rob, picking
fights with him and gradually cutting off the friendship. At
home, Alex and his sister had more than the usual brother/
sister fights, and loud, angry confrontations between him
and his father became almost a nightly routine. Once Alex
was so angry that he punched his bedroom wall with his
fists until he had made several holes.

One night a week before the anniversary of his mother's
death, Alex had a huge blowout with his father. He kept
arguing with his father over a minor incident. Finally, in a
rage, he grabbed a kitchen knife and challenged his father
to a fight. Alex's father took the knife away and sent Alex
to his room to "cool down."

Alex did not stay in his room. He climbed out the window,
taking a hunting knife that he kept hidden under his mat-
tress. Alex was so tired and angry that he didn't want to

pretend anymore. He was tired of living and made an attempt on his life.

In this chapter we will discuss what parents should do if their child or adolescent makes a serious attempt at suicide, is making suicidal gestures or threats, or is in a crisis state. It is not our intention to write a self-help book for parents to handle a suicidal child or adolescent or to provide parents with a therapy plan. An at-risk child or adolescent needs immediate professional help. What we hope to do is to provide a mental road map of actions that a parent can follow until professional help is available. In any situation where there are thoughts or a risk of suicide, even when you're not sure, *the first rule is to contact a mental health professional immediately.*

Intervention Overview

Although each family is unique, common guidelines are available to families in dealing with a suicidal child or adolescent. Also, though each child or adolescent is an individual, there are thoughts, feelings, and behaviors common to each and every one.

Strange as it may sound, both ambivalence and rigidity are present in suicidal children or adolescents. The ambivalence is about dying. They don't want to die, but they can't keep living with the emotional pain. The rigidity is due to black-and-white vision; these young people can't see any way out of their emotional pain except death. They are unable to solve a problem except with death. To the suicidal child or adolescent, death is the only choice. This combination of ambivalence and rigidity makes it of the utmost importance that someone intervene. But how does one intervene? Remember, the first rule is to contact a mental health professional.

Within each child or adolescent, there are three levels that need to be understood; this understanding makes it easier for you to recognize the signals and to cope. These levels are the emotional, the thinking, and the physical; when someone is upset, all three levels are affected. The emotional and the physical levels are probably the easiest to recognize when they are out of balance. Emotional imbalance can be seen and heard in anger, anxiety, worry, depression, or panic. The physical is seen in a variety of ways; perhaps there is pacing back and forth, withdrawal, destruction of property, or sleep and/or appetite changes. There usually is an aimless, impulsive need to react or to take some kind of action. The thinking level is harder to recognize. A person can't think straight. Thoughts are confused and jumbled; concentration is difficult, if not impossible.

What occurs in an at-risk youth is a change in behavior pattern. The child or adolescent is tense and unable to wait; he or she wants something to happen right now! The more tense, angry, and/or anxious these youths become, the more confused they are. They experience flip-flops in emotions, moods, and thoughts. They make mistakes in their thinking as their emotions begin to overwhelm them. Their problem-solving and coping skills become ineffectual; they are in a crisis state.

As stated previously, the following sections will provide you with some guidelines but should not take the place of professional help. *The first rule is always to seek professional help.*

Determining the Risk of Suicide

How do you know if your child or adolescent is thinking of or planning to commit suicide? The best way to determine the answer is to assess the risk level. Keep in mind that your youngster may deny his or her feelings or thoughts, or may not want to talk about them with you. If this is the case, perhaps your child would be more comfortable talking with someone else—if not a professional, someone he or she trusts and relates to. Regardless of the individual, the following nine issues should be considered. Don't be afraid to share these with that person.

1. Is your child or adolescent having suicidal thoughts, feelings, or intentions?

2. Is there a detailed plan?
3. How readily available is the method?
4. Is there a set time to commit suicide?
5. How likely is it that someone will interrupt the attempt?
6. Is there drug and/or alcohol involvement?
7. Has there been a previous suicide attempt?
8. How supportive is your child's or adolescent's environment?
9. How great is your child's or adolescent's anxiety/frustration level?

Let's look at these points in greater detail.

Is your child or adolescent having suicidal thoughts, feelings, or intentions? The American Association of Suicidology gives the following suggestions for approaching a person who is suspected of having suicidal thoughts, feelings, or intent.[1]

Don't be afraid to ask the questions. You are not going to put the thought into your child's head. Start off with a statement like this: "You appear to be kind of down." If the response is positive, ask whether he or she is feeling somewhat depressed. If that answer is yes, respond with a statement such as "I guess sometimes it seems as though it's not worth it to go on struggling and fighting when so many disappointing things happen to you." After a "yes" answer, one might ask, "Do you sometimes wake up in the morning wishing you were dead?" Finally you might ask a question such as "Have you been thinking about killing yourself?" Ease into asking about suicide in a caring and concerned way. A "yes" answer here, or even a veiled "yes," should be cause for concern and continued questions.

When there are negative responses or a hesitancy to discuss thoughts or feelings of suicide, our approach is to change the topic temporarily and to talk about other things that may be of interest to the youth. Once the child or adolescent begins to feel more relaxed and more comfortable, we go back to the subject. We continue doing this until we get an idea of the risk level.

Is there a detailed plan? A child or an adolescent who has a plan for suicide is at high risk, especially if the plan is detailed. If your child or adolescent has indicated that he or she is thinking about killing himself or herself or has the intent to do so, ask questions such as "How would you kill yourself?" "Do you have a plan?" "How would you go about killing yourself?"

For example, an adolescent has confided to a friend that she is thinking about shooting herself and has stolen the keys to her father's gun cabinet. If intent is established and if the youth has a specific plan, risk may be high.

How readily available is the method? If your child or adolescent has the method available or easily accessible, the risk is higher. Examples are the child who says that he intends to shoot himself and that guns are available to him, or an adolescent who wants to use carbon monoxide when a car is available.

If your child or adolescent has the intent, a specific plan, and the means to complete the suicide, the risk is extremely high.

Is there a set time to commit suicide? Time is an important factor; if one sets a time for the suicide attempt, risk must be considered high. If the time selected allows your child or adolescent to be alone for a period of time with no expected interruptions, completion of suicide is more possible. Because many suicide attempts by children and adolescents are made from after school until late at night, any suggested time within this period is to be considered serious, especially if no one will be home. For example, the girl who stole the keys to her father's gun cabinet plans to commit suicide on a weekend when her parents are away.

If your child has suicidal intent, a specific plan, the means to complete the act, and a set time, he or she must be considered a serious risk.

How likely is it that someone will interrupt the attempt? Children and adolescents know the expected schedule of family members, as well as the plans of close friends. Any plan that allows for a suicide attempt when no one is expected to interrupt, or in which the method allows no intervention, is to be considered serious. There is less chance of an intervention for the girl who plans to shoot herself than for the boy who plans to use carbon monoxide at a time when family members may be expected home.

If your child or adolescent expresses an intent to commit suicide, has a specific plan, has the means to complete the act, and has the time set so no one can interrupt, he or she is, an extremely serious risk.

Is there drug or alcohol involvement? Drugs and alcohol act to make a child or an adolescent more impulsive and reduce the youth's control over his or her own behavior. They also lessen the fear of death and encourage risk taking.

Given the use of these substances by any child or adolescent who is contemplating suicide, and given a number of other signs, you must consider the risk extreme.

Has there been a previous suicide attempt? Any previous attempt at suicide should suggest that suicide is seen as one option to solve a problem. Consider behaviors that might be self-harming but are not viewed as a specific suicide attempt, such as an "accidental" overdose of medication, a one-car accident, frequent overuse of alcohol and/or drugs, or playing dangerous games.

If the option is in place—an option that we feel will persist in future years but perhaps not as priority behavior—the risk increases when some of the other signs are seen as well.

How supportive is your child's or adolescent's environment? Many children and adolescents who think about and attempt suicide feel isolated and alone. If youths have few friends or cannot appreciate the friends they have, or if they have few, if any, significant relationships with peers or adults, and if other signs are also seen, there is a risk of suicide.

The more one is alone and isolated and the more other risk factors appear, the more serious the risk.

How great is your child's or adolescent's anxiety/frustration level? The higher your child's or adolescent's anxiety level and the greater his or her frustration, the more likely it is that the youth will use desperate means to relieve his or her feelings.

The risk of suicide increases when a high anxiety or frustration level is seen in combination with other factors. The child or adolescent who becomes unreasonably angry at minor irritations or who is easily frustrated and quite impulsive should be carefully evaluated.

In summary, please keep in mind that not all of the above signs have to be seen to put a child or adolescent at risk. Even one sign should trigger enough concern to talk with your child and/or to refer him or her to a mental health professional.

Crisis

Crisis is a temporary state of upset and disorganization. The youth is unable to solve a problem or perhaps even to cope with minor day-to-day demands and responsibilities. The child or adolescent who is in a crisis state, with suicidal feelings, is or feels unable to handle circumstances that are overwhelming to him or her at that time. Thoughts, threats, or even an attempt at suicide are the only way out that that young person can see. What can the family do? What action should be taken or not taken?

The conflicting feelings and the resulting confusion that occur within the family when a child or an adolescent is in a crisis state are so overwhelming that ineffectual actions are often the result. It is clear, however, that you need to reestablish some coping abilities as quickly as possible.[2] The longer the crisis is allowed to continue, the more difficult it is to intervene.

Make contact. Although this is easier to say than to do, try not to be disturbed by your child's or adolescent's feelings—distress, anger, depression, or whatever else. Try to bring a feeling of calm confidence into the situation. Your child or adolescent does not need to think that the crisis is so hopeless that even you, an adult, are overwhelmed.

Encourage your child or adolescent to talk. Show your concern. Practice your active listening skills (see chapter 8). Accept what is being said. Although it is not necessary to accept your child's view, you must accept the feelings that are being expressed. Do not make a judgment.

Don't expect to have all the answers. It's OK if you don't know something. Just listen and focus on your child's or adolescent's feelings; this behavior will reflect your interest and concern. Keep him or her talking; if you don't understand something, say you don't understand. Have your child talk; then have him or her talk more, and more after that.

Remember that nonverbal communication is also a way of sharing the pain and upset, especially when you do not know what to say or when there are no words that can be said. Nonverbal communication could be stroking your child's or adolescent's hair, touching the arm or back, or putting your arm around his or her shoulder. Sharing food or drink or taking a walk together are examples of nonintrusive support.

Try to learn what happened. Try to find out what caused the crisis. Suicide does not happen spontaneously; there is a buildup of stressors with which your child or adolescent cannot cope. Often adults see the precipitating event as something minor and as the only reason why the child or adolescent wants to die. In reality, however, the precipitating event is the "straw that broke the camel's back." This "straw" needs to be identified so that the anxiety can be at least partially reduced.

Find out what happened. When did it happen? Who was involved? Have your child or adolescent tell the story.

Don't be surprised if your child or adolescent is confused or even vague when telling his or her story. You may have a hard time following the conversation, trying to sort out who the characters are, or even understanding what the story is all about. Although your child or adolescent is confused or vague about what's happened, he or she will be rigid regarding how the problem can be solved. Comments such as "Nothing works," "It's hopeless," or "No one can help" reflect your child's or adolescent's overfocusing on the problem and inability to see the alternatives. Often death is the only choice that the youth sees.

It is important that you, the listener, not be drawn into your child's pattern of overfocusing. Define the reality of the situation for your child. When someone is in a crisis state of confusion and disorganization, everything looks overwhelming and hopeless. Try to sort out the issues by time. What's the issue that needs immediate attention? What issue can wait? An example of an immediate need is a safe place to spend the night. Later needs might be getting a job and receiving counseling.

When the crisis event is identified, it will help your child or adolescent to focus his or her thoughts. When you summarize the crisis event for your child, you give the message of concern and caring.

Examine the choices. Although your child or adolescent needs help in looking at solutions to a problem, he or she always needs to be involved in solving that problem. This involvement gives your child a feeling of control and competency. Don't rush in with a solution. Typically it will be rejected with reasons why it is unworkable. You will receive comments that begin with "Yes, but. . ." Wait to give advice or offer solutions until the anxiety or anger is lessened. Remember, advice and/or solutions that are given too early will be rejected. Also, you will alienate the child by giving the message that you don't know what's going on or that you're not listening to him or her, just like everyone else.

First, have your child or adolescent tell what he or she has already tried. Next try to have him or her come up with other solutions or different approaches to solutions already attempted. Because of overwhelming emotions you might have to guide your child or adolescent into producing other ideas. You might ask, for example, "What would happen if you told your boyfriend? Called your friend? Left the party?"

Only after your child or adolescent has told you what has been tried and has attempted to come up with suggestions should you join in with alternative solutions. You could begin with "What do you think about coming home tonight? Contacting school?" and so on.

You also need to help your child or adolescent examine obstacles to the plan. It is important that the obstacles be identified and talked about. Again, you should emphasize that the current upset may interfere with his or her thinking, and so you must try to foresee possible obstacles to a plan. You might say, for example, "Suppose your father won't let you in the house." In reviewing obstacles, it would help the child or adolescent if you tried "practice runs" together: "If my father won't let me in, then I'll call my sister and ask if I can stay there for the night." When a plan is unworkable because the obstacles have not been explored, your child's feelings that nothing works or that it's hopeless are confirmed.

Take action. With a high-risk child or adolescent the adult needs to take control. This could mean anything: calling for emergency help, making arrangements for counseling, or saying, "I am concerned for you and I may take this action" or "We need to talk." By acting directly and in a positive manner, you can respond to the youth's confusion, ambivalence, and rigidity of thought.

Set the boundaries and limits by establishing rules. Be very concrete with plans. Examples of actions are taking away the pills (gun, car keys), making an appointment, or driving the youth to the hospital.

When the risk is lower (with no danger to self or others) and when your child or adolescent is able to act on his or her own behalf, you can help by aiding him or her in taking an action to solve a problem. For example, encourage your son or daughter to make those important phone calls or contacts on his or her own, such as the call to AA or to the boyfriend or girlfriend to end a bad relationship.

Build a support network. Your child or adolescent may resist contact with other people, but the more contacts he or she has, the better. Isolation is to be avoided. There is a need to involve others—siblings, friends, teachers, anyone your son or daughter may use for support. It is important that everyone helps. Support from a meaningful network may mean the difference between coping or collapsing under pressure.

When your child requests secrecy, try to find out why. Usually the youth is afraid that others will think that he or she is "crazy." Try to be reassuring. The upset, confusion, and helplessness are not mental illness but a normal reaction to an unusual happening.

Tell your child or adolescent that talking about his or her suicidal feelings and thoughts was the right thing to do. Do this very concretely; say, for example, "I'm glad you told me. It was the right thing to do." This statement removes any feelings of guilt and embarrassment that your child or adolescent might be feeling.

Always remember to get professional help.

Guidelines for a Variety of Situations

An Emergency Life-threatening Attempt

Mary is a fourteen-year-old freshman in high school. She is an only child; her parents were divorced approximately three years ago. When the divorce became final, Mary's mother thought that Mary might become depressed or angry over the divorce. Instead she found that Mary was "overly good and always trying to say and do the right thing." Then, in recent months, Mary changed. She began to drink, smoke pot, and have a sexual relationship with a twenty-year-old dropout. In school, Mary cut classes and failed almost all her subjects.

Mary's mother tried talking to her, and Mary always promised to try to do better. She said, "I fell in with the wrong crowd at school, and I will never do any of that again. All I want is to have you trust me again."

For about six months Mary seem to be doing OK. There were still upsets at home, but overall Mary's mother thought the worst was over. In reality, however, Mary was keeping up a double life, trying to convince her mother that "everything's perfect, and you can trust me" while she continued her pot smoking and sexual activities.

Mary made a serious suicide attempt by drug overdose in her mother's bedroom. Her mother had a date that evening but came home much earlier than expected. At first she did not realize what was wrong, and thought Mary had fallen asleep on her bed. When she realized that Mary had overdosed, panic set in. She called a neighbor who was a nurse. The neighbor called the ambulance and got Mary to the hospital.

When Mary regained consciousness, it was learned that her best friend, Debbie, who had known that Mary was thinking about killing herself, had given her the pills. The social worker at the hospital contacted Debbie, who was filled with guilt and confusion over her part in Mary's attempted suicide. Mary had made Debbie promise not to tell anyone, and Debbie had kept her promise.

Mary, her mother, and her father entered therapy together; only in this way could Mary's anger and depression over the divorce be worked out.

In a life-threatening situation, the central issue is the physical survival and safety not only of the child or adolescent, but of others as well. Do not attempt to handle a volatile situation by yourself; get outside help as quickly as possible. Depending on the severity of the action, outside help might require an emergency call to a 911 number or to an appropriate emergency number in your area for the police and/or an ambulance, or contacting a mental health professional or a hospital.

It is helpful to know the method that the child or adolescent used. In case of a drug overdose, the drug or type of drug, the amount taken, the approximate time of ingestion, and the youth's weight are important facts.

When a child or adolescent is suicidal and is unable to control self-destructive impulses, hospitalization is strongly recommended.

Such a serious action always requires follow-up family

counseling by a trained professional. All too often after an attempt has been made, the seriousness of the behavior is denied, both by the parents and even at times by the youth. Parents may find the thought that their child attempted suicide too frightening to handle. A youth may talk openly about his or her suicide attempt to someone in a hospital emergency room, only to change the story to "it was an accident" when parents arrive on the scene.

We saw an example of denial recently in our practice. A fourteen-year-old girl was referred to us by a hospital emergency room after taking an overdose of her insulin. The girl had recently had an abortion at the insistence of her boyfriend. In the emergency room she admitted the suicide attempt. The emergency room staff informed the parents of the attempt, but when the parents talked with their daughter, she denied it. She explained that she simply forgot that she had already taken her morning insulin, and took a double dose. She continued to deny the attempt even in the therapy sessions, to a point where her parents were convinced that therapy was not needed.

A Nonemergency Life-threatening Attempt

Betty is a fifteen-year-old girl who was abandoned by her mother when she was ten months of age. Her stepmother of twelve years is the only mother she has ever known or can remember.

Recently Betty asked her stepmother for two-hundred dollars, and became angry when her stepmother refused. At first Betty refused to say why she wanted the money, commenting only that if her stepmother really loved and trusted her, she would give her the money. It was later discovered that Betty wanted the money because she thought she was pregnant by her best friend's twenty-four-year-old boyfriend. Betty planned to give the money to the boy so that he would "really like her." If she did not get the money, and so get this boy to like her and stand by her, she planned to kill herself.

Betty did have a suicide plan: she was planning to kill

herself with carbon monoxide. She had the means available: the keys to her stepmother's car. She had decided on a time: after school, before her stepmother returned home from work.

During an emotion-packed conversation with her stepmother, Betty revealed that she had made a previous suicide attempt some months ago, cutting her wrist with a razor blade after carving a boy's initials into her arm. At that time Betty's younger sister had stopped the attempt. Betty felt that she really was going to kill herself, and that she would make sure no one was around this time.

Feeling that Betty was quite serious and capable of killing herself, the stepmother kept a watch on Betty and called her husband to come home as quickly as possible. Upon the father's arrival, it was decided that Betty needed to be hospitalized because of her overwhelming despair and her feelings that she was not wanted or loved and that no one would miss her if she wasn't around. Betty steadfastly maintained that no one could stop her from killing herself. She felt that the "family has to sleep sometime; they can't watch me twenty-four hours a day."

Betty was admitted to the local hospital's psychiatric ward. After her dismissal from the hospital, the family continued in therapy. A year later, the future appeared promising for Betty.

In a child or adolescent who is at a high risk for suicide, the lethality is high or the youth is unable to cope or to act on his or her own behalf. Again, outside professional help is necessary.

There is a need to implement safety guidelines. Try to determine the method and the means of the planned attempt. If the child or adolescent possesses the means to commit suicide, try to have him or her surrender it. Do not hesitate to lock up pills, guns, knives, or other sharp objects. It is always amazing to us that a parent will bring in a child or adolescent who has planned a suicide but has not thought to remove the means of suicide from the home. If the child or adolescent possesses a weapon, do not hesitate to ask for police aid. Common sense should prevail. Keep in mind your own safety and the safety of others.

Until professional help is available, there will be a need to set a watch on the child or adolescent. This means that the youth should not be left alone. Someone must be with him or her at all times. This action obviously puts a strain on all family members, but it must be done. Hospitalization may be necessary and may be the most logical course of action.

Anna was a seventeen-year-old girl who was threatening to kill herself over a broken relationship. Before the breakup, Anna had carved her boyfriend's initials into her arm, scratched her face, and pulled out hunks of her hair. Unfortunately there was no room at the hospital, so she had to stay at home until a bed was available. In view of her inability to control her actions, Anna needed to be watched continually because of the high risk of suicide. Her parents removed all pills, knives, and scissors from the house, as well as any other possible means of harm. They took turns monitoring Anna until she could be admitted to the hospital.

Possible Suicide

Jeff is a seventeen-year-old honor roll high school student. He participates in various extracurricular activities and is well liked by teachers and peers. Jeff expected to attend an Ivy League university, but recent family financial difficulties have made that unlikely unless he wins a substantial scholarship. In an attempt to help his family, Jeff took a part-time job after school, but this caused his grades to drop dramatically. His parents have recently separated; his mother has a serious heart condition.

Jeff's girlfriend of two years recently asked that they be "just friends" so that she can date other people. In order to "prove" his friendship, Jeff gave her his whole tape collection and all his old pictures of the two of them together.

Because he was concerned about Jeff, a favorite teacher tried to spend some time talking to him about future plans. Jeff's responses were so unlike him that the teacher decided to call Jeff's father.

Jeff was angry that his teacher had interfered in his business, and refused to talk to his father. Jeff began to open up only when his father insisted that he and Jeff go together to talk to someone about all the losses in their lives. Jeff spoke of his feeling that it was not worth getting up in the morning. He had thought of killing himself but was concerned about how this would affect his mother's health. Although he did not have a definite plan, he had a time picked out. His mother was going out of state to visit her sister; Jeff felt that would be an "ideal time" because "there would be someone with her when she got the news." His giving away of the records and pictures was his way of saying good-bye to his girlfriend and sparing his mother the "trouble of clearing out my junk."

Jeff, his mother, and his father entered therapy. His parents eventually were divorced, but Jeff was able to handle the situation and get on with his own life.

The child or adolescent who sees suicide as a possibility and is considering it is regarded as a moderate risk. In this case the youth has the desire to die, but may not have the means and has not made a concrete plan. There are family and friends around, and the child or adolescent is handling day-to-day problems—maybe not very well, but still with some ability to cope.

In dealing with a child or adolescent who threatens or makes a suicidal gesture or attempt, we stress again the need to get professional help.

There is very little difference between a suicidal gesture and an attempt with regard to whether counseling should be initiated. In a gesture, the child or adolescent may not really mean to carry through the action, or there may be no "life-threatening" results. An example of a gesture is a superficial scratching or cutting of the wrists. In an attempt, a more determined action to end an emotional pain is undertaken. Both the gesture and the attempt are definite cries for help and attention, and must be acted on quickly. Professional help is strongly recommended.

Mary Ann was a nine-year-old girl who lived with her mother, stepfather, and younger sister. There was a great deal of conflict between her mother and her stepfather. As arguments became more frequent, Mary Ann became increasingly withdrawn, behavioral problems began, and schoolwork deteriorated. Mary Ann, taking a sash from her mother's robe, tied one end around her neck and the other around the post of her bunk bed. Then she sat and waited for her mother to come and tuck her in. Was this a serious suicide attempt? Whether it was an attempt or a gesture, it was a definite cry for help. The family did enter therapy and completed it successfully.

The Low-Risk Child or Adolescent

Stacy is a ten-year-old girl whose parents have had marital difficulties and have separated several times. As Stacy says, "They are getting revorced again." Stacy's overall appearance is one of dishevelment and neglect. She has stolen from her mother's pocketbook. She is not liked by her schoolmates and is frequently taunted by them. Her father is easily angered with Stacy because she is "clingy and whiny." Lately Stacy has started masturbating while watching television.

Stacy frequently talked to her older, married sister about how sad she was and how "everything was messed up and couldn't ever get better." Stacy felt that her grandmother, who had died the year before, "had it lucky 'cause she don't have to worry no more." Stacy said she wished she could "be up in heaven too."

The low-risk child or adolescent has vague feelings of not wanting to go on, with a sense of helplessness and hopelessness. There are no plans for suicide; no threats have been made. It is possible, however, that the youth might develop such overwhelming feelings and that suicide could become a possibility. This type of child or adolescent would benefit from counseling. Helping the low-risk child or adolescent to learn how to solve problems and to cope is an important task. For such youths, expressions of concern and caring may prevent a rise to a higher risk level.

The suicidal child or adolescent needs to know that someone is concerned about his or her well-being, and that someone is listening, understands, and is accepting of them. Encourage him or her to talk. Listen to the facts and recognize the feelings. When the anger, depression, and anxiety are recognized, the emotional intensity is reduced.

When you offer a solution to a problem, do not be surprised if it is rejected. This rejection means that the youth needs to continue talking and is not yet ready for problem solving. The feeling, whether it is anger, depression, anxiety, or any combination, is too strong. The emotional intensity still needs to be reduced; this is best accomplished by having the youth talk.

It would be beneficial to make the child's school aware of your concern. (The support network that is available through the school, of course, varies not only from state to state but also from school to school within the same district.) In our experience, the more outreach is available for the youth and the parents, the better.

Remember that at-risk children or adolescents need professional help. They may need help on an emergency basis, or there may be time to select an appropriate course of action. To prepare for an emergency, know or have immediately available the telephone numbers not only for police, fire, and ambulance services but also for a suicide or crisis hot line in your area. A 911 or similar emergency number may be appropriate for a suicide in process but not for gaining insight into suicide or for obtaining step-by-step help for a near-crisis state. Look in your telephone book under possible sources of help, such as suicide hotline, infoline, mental health, counseling, psychotherapy, psychologists, psychiatrists, counselors, crisis line, or hospital clinics.

Remember that all mental health workers may not be trained in or experienced with suicide. Make contact with any appropriate source of help and ask specifically if they are qualified. Keep any referral sources' telephone numbers handy; do not hesitate to use them if you have any concern. Remember, it's better to overreact and to appear overanxious or overconcerned than to take a chance with your child's life.

Dos and Don'ts of Suicide

Do take all threats seriously.	Don't ignore or explain away suicidal comments.
Do notice signs of depression and withdrawal.	Don't explain away sudden behavior changes.
Do be concerned if there is a loss of a loved one, even a pet, or a loss of self-esteem.	Don't think that a youth will get over it.
Do trust your own judgment.	Don't be misled.
Do tell others.	Don't keep a confidence or worry that you might be overreacting or look silly.
Do express your concerns to the youth.	Don't sermonize, moralize, or use guilt tactics.
Do stay with the youth if there is a crisis.	Don't assume that the youth will be all right alone.
Do, if safety permits, remove the means of suicide.	Don't leave the means of suicide available to the youth.
Do seek professional help.	Don't handle the situation yourself.
Do become involved in therapy.	Don't assume that just because the youth is seeing someone for help, your support is not necessary, needed, or wanted.

11

After the Suicide Attempt

A SUICIDAL act, whether it is attempted and completed or attempted and not completed, certainly suggests that something has gone wrong for the youth who made the attempt. Possibly, among other things, he or she has experienced difficulty in his or her school life, social life, and/or family life. Regardless of the cause, the act suggests that the family was not able to give that youth the support and protection he or she needed and wanted. For whatever reason, death by suicide seems to cause more problems than death by most other causes. Whether the attempted suicide succeeds or fails, you need to be aware of some of the reactions that are seen in many parents.

One of the first reactions to the news that your son or daughter has attempted suicide is denial. It's difficult to accept the fact that a child of yours could have attempted such an act. You'll also feel anger; that anger could be directed at almost anyone who attempts suicide, not only your child. You may also feel a general fear that your child has the capacity to self-destruct. Although this fear will lessen over the years, it will remain as an uncomfortable and possibly unrecognized feeling of anxiety, especially in a crisis.

Most likely you will feel some shame and guilt over the attempted suicide. The shame may result from the fact that suicide is still not an acceptable way of dying. People still have difficulty dealing with this form of death, almost as if death from suicide is different from death in any other way.

They don't know how to respond; they won't know what to say or how to say it, and the stigma attached to an attempted suicide is much the same as for a completed suicide.

Parents of children or adolescents who commit suicide are usually seen more negatively by society than parents of those who die from illness or accidents. Youths who attempt or complete suicide are often seen as coming from disturbed homes. The parents of these children are often seen as being emotionally disturbed. Although this belief may or may not be true, people in general reflect these feelings, and parents of children who attempt suicide should be aware of them.

Almost without exception, most parents of children or adolescents who attempt or complete suicide will feel guilt. The guilt stems from what they, as parents, could have done to prevent the attempt or the suicide, and from what they did that could have caused it. Parents, especially fathers, may tend to blame things outside the family for the attempt or the suicide. Such factors as friends, society in general, school stress, and/or drugs and alcohol are often blamed. There is also a tendency to explain the attempt or the suicide as an accident.

Our experience in private practice with depressed and suicidal youths suggests that many family factors increase the possibility of suicide. Often the interaction between suicidal youths and their parents shows serious failure in communication and understanding. There is unhappiness and discontent. Parents' expectations of their children, especially in school, are often unreasonable. Discipline is poor, nonexistent, or at best ineffective. Parents often use a wide variety of techniques in trying to deal with the problems. Nagging, yelling, and criticizing are most often cited by children and adolescents. Many youths who attempt suicide have difficulty in their relationships with their parents. Often the relationship that is most disturbed is with the parent of the opposite sex. Lack of a warm relationship among family members may be as much a factor as actual conflict.[1] The parents themselves may be unhappy and discontented in their relationship and may not enjoy family life. Very often the parents were not good models of adjustment for the children. Because suicidal children and adolescents, more than nonsuicidal youths, seem unconsciously to take in the characteristics, ideas, and feelings of another person, poor role models increase their feelings of negative self-worth. This situation could increase the risk of suicide.

If the above is true, "business as usual" after a suicide attempt will increase the likelihood of another, possibly successful attempt. There is no reason to believe that anything will change simply because of a suicide attempt. We can expect changes to take place only if parents are convinced that they have a part in any suicide or suicide attempt. But what kind of changes? Who has to change? How long will it take? We can suggest the kind of changes and we can tell you who has to change, but no one can tell you how long it will take. Much depends on how seriously damaged the family and the relationships are and on the strength of the motivation for change.

Attempted suicide is a cry for help. It is often aimed at adjusting life rather than ending it. It is a cry for attention, but not in as simple a manner as it seems. The attention the suicidal youth needs is caring, support, and protection. The irony is that after his or her attempt the attempter encounters generally negative attitudes from almost all segments of society, even including the medical personnel who treat him or her. The implication here is that even stronger family support is needed.

You should realize, however, that suicide or attempted suicide is often due to conflict with a certain individual. That individual could be a parent, a sibling, a relative, or a friend, among others. If it is a parent or a sibling, that is all the more reason for change and understanding in the family. Parents must attempt to see some of the behavior of a suicide attempter as signs of unhappiness and discontent, but often they see these behaviors only as problems that need to be stopped.

Many people, children and adolescents included, survive a suicide attempt only to deny that it was such an attempt. This is often what parents want to hear; if they can convince themselves that it was an "accident," they see no reason for any professional intervention. Regardless of how they feel, however, any youth who is involved in a life-threatening situation should be seen and evaluated by a mental health professional. Because the parents and the family play a part in any suicide attempt, the family should also be seen and evaluated. The attempted suicide is a signal that something within the family is wrong; unless change takes place, in all probability there will be other attempts and possibly success. We don't mean to imply that parents and/or family are the sole cause of a suicide attempt, but they are a strong means of support and identification. Young people do not grow up in a vacuum; their lives are very much influenced by parents and siblings as well as by relatives and friends. For this reason parents and family members are involved in the therapeutic process.

Whether or not parents involve themselves and their children in therapy, changes in the family must take place. Any time is a good time to start, but a suicide attempt offers a special opportunity because everyone involved is aware of the seriousness of what happened. In most cases they are eager to see that it doesn't happen again.

Possible Areas for Change

Communication

Many parents ask, "What do I say to a son or daughter who has attempted suicide?" Try a simple "I love you and I want to understand what happened." Encourage your child to do most of the talking. Let him or her tell you what's wrong. Let them talk about their feelings and problems while you *listen*. Accept what they say without trying to defend yourself or your spouse. Don't—we repeat, *don't*—tell children how lucky they are to have what they have, or what they have to look forward to, or how much they have hurt the ones they love. All this does is add to the guilt over having made a suicide attempt. If enough stress is created, it will help ensure another, possibly successful, attempt. Remember that a suicide attempt is a negative form of behavioral communication. When people fail at verbal communication, they may attempt behavioral communication, one form of which is suicide.

Voice your acceptance of your child's feelings. Follow the good communication suggestions given in chapter 8; stay away from "why," "you," and "we" statements. All these statements do is put young people on the defensive and close down communication. Here are some examples of these types of statement:

"Why did you try to kill yourself?" This question assumes that the child has a relatively simple answer, when in reality the answer may be quite complex and difficult to put into words. It puts the child on the defensive because the question implies that there is *a* reason, when in fact there could be many reasons.

"You make me so angry" will certainly lead to defensiveness because you're putting all the blame on your child. This statement places responsibility for what has happened onto the child and frees you from any part in the process.

"We can't do things like that!" tells your child or adolescent that you're speaking for him or her and implies that children have no say in their own feelings.

Of vital importance is the need to communicate accurately. In many cases, parents and their children come away from a conversation or simple communication with two different ideas of what is expected. One way to avoid this problem is to repeat important aspects of your conversation and to clarify your child's position by repeating what you understand him or her to be saying.

It is also important that after an attempted suicide you respond to your child in a calm, even-tempered manner. Keep your rate of speech equal to that of the person you're talking to; keep your volume at a conversational level. Try not to talk in a harsh tone but in a tone that will calm the child. Keep eye contact comfortable; try to stay fairly close to the child or adolescent with nothing between you, such as a table or desk.

In general, communication must express to your children

that you care and understand, and that you can help them if they will allow you.

Reality

As in a completed suicide, parents will feel guilt when their children make an attempt on their life. You may think it's your fault, and will find many reasons to convince yourself that it is. If only you had been there for them or had spent more time with them. If only you had noticed some of the behaviors that were signs of trouble. This list could go on and on, but it would fail to take into consideration an important fact: Most parents do what they think is right, not only for themselves but also for their family. We have never seen parents who deliberately do something to cause their children harm. You will usually do what you think is right at the time and then live with the consequences, whether positive or negative. There is no guilt or blame to be attached. This is not to say that there are not good reasons to feel guilt in some cases. When you have a serious problem but fail to deal with it and allow it to interfere with your relationships, you must live with the consequences of your failure to act. And when you behave in a manner that you know is not appropriate and that affects others negatively, the guilt must be dealt with.

Expectations

Parents often have unrealistic expectations of their children. You must look at your suicide attempter realistically in terms of strengths and weaknesses. Your child or adolescent will have good points and bad points; usually you will find it easier to verbalize and accept the good points than the bad points, or vice versa. What can you realistically expect from your child in terms of school grades, social behavior, home behavior, chores, attitude, siblings, and emotions, among other things? If you can accept the fact that your children will have good days and bad days and that they will exhibit a full range of human emotions, including anger, you will have a more realistic view. You must accept their intellectual and behavioral limitations. Children are not little adults! They are children growing to be adults; to guide them successfully you must have a realistic grasp of their intelligence, emotions, and capabilities. Goals and expectations should be geared to their age and capacity.

Another aspect of expectations is expecting too little of your children. Here you may tend to move in and solve problems for your children rather than allow the situation to be a learning experience for them. The more you can allow them to solve their problems, the more secure they will be as they grow older. You may be a parent who has difficulty letting go; thus you've developed a child who can't function independently. It's not too late to develop a trust in your child's ability to solve problems. Allow them the opportunity to solve their own problems, letting them know that they have your support and help, if necessary. Obviously you must use good judgment in deciding what your child can or cannot handle. You must set appropriate limits and boundaries.

Anger

One of the most difficult emotions for parents to accept is anger. Yet if your child committed or attempted suicide, anger was present for both you and the child. You, like many parents, may have wanted to see only happy emotions from your child; consequently, in many ways, you did not allow anger to surface. But anger that surfaces and is dealt with is not pushed down and allowed to fester. In suicidal youths, the anger is very likely to be expressed against themselves. If they do express it outwardly, most likely it will be directed at you, the parent, who has been responsible for meeting his or her needs. Children and adolescents have learned that anger is not acceptable; now they must be able to learn that it can be expressed, but only in acceptable ways. We often say to children and adolescents when we see them in therapy that it's permissible to show their anger at us, but we make conditions. If they choose to stamp their feet, clench their fists, walk out of the office and slam the door, or express their anger verbally, it's acceptable. If they choose to throw a chair through the window to express their anger, that act is not acceptable.

Feelings of Rejection

When children or adolescents reach the point of attempting suicide, they feel that they have been abandoned by everyone, especially their parents. Your child has depended on you for guidance and support, understanding, and acceptance. Seemingly they have learned that they can't approach you or trust you to deal with their problems. Perhaps that wouldn't be too bad if you were able to approach them, but in many cases parents can't approach their children and children can't approach their parents. If they have been taught that people can't approach other people whether or not they have problems, they will feel isolated, rejected, and abandoned. Young suicide attempters often see their parents as rejecting. They feel as if they have no one at home to talk with. You need to encourage open communication, both verbal and nonverbal, if you expect your son or daughter to feel accepted. Let them know you are available to talk. Make yourself available, even if only for a walk or a game. Let them know in no uncertain terms how much you love them and want to be there for them. Isolation is to be avoided at all costs because it reinforces the feelings of rejection and abandonment. Stay close and let them know you care.

Hope

If your child has committed suicide or has made a suicidal attempt, in all probability he or she was feeling a sense of hopelessness. The cause of this feeling is their inability to deal with their life stresses. They don't see any way out of any uncomfortable situation. They don't see any way of changing any of life's circumstances. The more hopeless and helpless they feel, the more likely they are to be depressed. The more depressed they feel, the more likely they are to feel hopeless and helpless. Your child must be helped to see that life and conditions can change. Yet even the thought of change may frighten them because they feel as unsure of handling change as they do of handling present circumstances. As parents, you know that time will take care of some of their problems, but time is something that adolescents in particular don't feel they have. They deal in the present. They want satisfaction and relief now. Often they see only two solutions to any problem: it stops or it continues. You, as parents, must help them to see that they need not always be unhappy and alone, that changes at home are possible, and that their relationships outside home can develop in a positive manner. How do you do this? By offering them hope through positive changes at home and in family relationships.

Why?

The question all people ask is "Why did the child or adolescent attempt or complete suicide?" Although there are no absolute reasons, our clinical experience leads us to believe that the reasons given to us by children and adolescents are surface explanations that hide serious feelings of loneliness and emptiness, and the sense that no one cares. The following reasons were given to us in our private practice by children and adolescents; these reasons are similar to those seen in recent research on overdose cases.[2] If you address these reasons with your child, at least you have an opening for making changes and developing better communications.

To Seek Help. This desperate attempt to get help suggests that you and others weren't there for your child. You need to help him or her to understand that you can and will help in any way possible. To help, however, means that they must communicate the need for help in ways that you can see and understand.

Some children and adolescents hesitate to approach their parents for help with their problems. They may not want to burden their parents, they may feel that their parents wouldn't understand, or experience has shown that their parents aren't available to them, either physically or emotionally. Explore with your children possible reasons for this hesitancy. Look at your own availability to them. Are you approachable? Do you have the time? Also explore other available resources for getting help with problems, such as school personnel, clergy, or close family friends.

To Escape from an Impossible Situation. The impossible situation could be at home, at school, or in the child's social life. It is necessary to explore what situation drove your child to make an attempt on his or her life. If it is within your power to remedy or at least alleviate the situation, that will remove some of the stress. Remember: what you may regard as a minor problem, the child or adolescent may see as an impossible situation. You need to help your child look at alternative ways of dealing with life's situations. Not all solutions are totally acceptable, but as long the child is dealing with them to the best of his or her ability, that's all anyone can reasonably expect. At best, your child will need to learn to compromise.

To Get Relief from a Terrible State of Mind. This motive suggests that your child is under considerable stress and confusion. These youths' emotional hurt is so overpowering that they are unable to see options realistically, and so they become confused. They need your help in handling the stress, perhaps by looking at their roles and responsibilities and ordering them by priority. Teach them to deal with important issues and to let the less important ones go. Help them to look at themselves and others realistically. Help them to see that no more is expected of them than is reasonable for them. Help them to confide in you or in someone with whom they can talk.

To Try to Influence Some Particular Person. This motive could be simply to gain love and acceptance from someone or to manipulate that person. The desire to gain love implies feelings of nonacceptance or a lack of recognition from a particular person or persons. All people need acceptance and recognition; children and adolescents are no different. This motive for an attempted suicide implies that the youth needs to be accepted or recognized as important in the eyes of a particular person. The child feels that only a suicide attempt will induce that person to fill some of his or her needs. These needs are varied, but may include love, caring, recognition, nurturance, support, or guidance. Parents can help by listening and assuring their children both verbally and nonverbally that they are loved and are recognized as unique individuals.

Threatening suicide as a way to change a person's mind is emotional blackmail. This is a control issue that needs to be resolved within the relationship itself or within the family unit. For relationships outside the family unit, clear statements—broken record statements—reduce false hope and place the responsibility back on the youth. To gain control within the family unit, set limits and maintain them with clearly defined statements.

To Show How Much They Loved Someone. This reason is often given when one person's love for another is not returned in the same manner or with the same intensity. Rejection is often felt, and the attempted suicide is aimed at gaining the desired love and acceptance. The sense of rejection only compounds or confirms the young person's low self-esteem and negative self-worth. Parents must recognize that the child's or adolescent's love for another person is a strong emotion, not to be denied or ridiculed. Understanding support given in a sympathetic manner provides the youth with a haven where healing can occur. Time and encouragement to stay active will help the healing process.

To Make Things Easier for Others. This reason suggests a feeling of negative self-worth within the child or adolescent. Such youths see their lives as relatively unimportant and expendable. They will sacrifice themselves for the welfare of others, and they believe that their death will resolve or make things easier for those remaining. In reality, however, their death only offers greater pain. These youths must be helped to see their importance to the family and to others. Parents need to encourage compassion and acceptance, along with clearly defined roles and expectations within the family for each family member. They must examine their own roles, responsibilities, and expectations. Have they abdicated their parental role and empowered their child with responsibilities beyond their capabilities? Do they expect more of their child than is reasonable?

To Make People Sorry. These youths attempt to punish or gain revenge on others for felt hurts or rejections; they want to pay back others for the way they were treated. Their anger is so intense that they see death as the only way of expressing their anger and of making others sorry. In reality, however, they are only punishing themselves.

This motive is another variation of emotional blackmail. Although parents need compassion in dealing with these young people, they also need to teach them appropriate ways of expressing or releasing anger. They need to know that anger is OK and is a common human emotion. It's not whether you get angry; it's how you express it.

To Frighten Someone or to Get Their Own Way. In an attempted suicide, this motive also amounts to emotional blackmail. It puts parents into a very difficult situation: if they give in to a child's or adolescent's demands under the threat of suicide, the child maintains control and can make almost any demand. If they don't give in, the child may attempt suicide and/or may succeed in killing himself or herself. The parents must help the child to see this dilemma from the parents' point of view and then must help him or her to find other alternatives to fill the needs. Again, we must emphasize that this is emotional blackmail. A threatened or attempted suicide is a way of controlling parents and others. This youth is saying, "Give me my own way or I will kill myself." The only way to handle this situation, both within the family and in other relationships, is to open communication, to set limits, and to keep those limits. Avoid mixed messages by giving clear, concise statements. Avoid continuing a discussion that places you in a defensive position. Continue the discussion only when anxieties and anger are diminished.

To Make People Understand How Desperate They Were Feeling. This is the last cry for help. Because previous signals were ignored, the child feels that there is no other way to get a person's attention. The young person's confusion often precludes any other avenue of choice or help. Such youths have no other way to show how desperate they feel. Once again, the parents must show their love and acceptance of the child, both verbally and behaviorally. They must help that child to see that they are there for him or her, but the child must communicate that need. Parents must not interpret suicidal behavior as merely a call for attention. They must not deny the seriousness of the situation.

To Find Out Whether They Are Really Loved. These young people are desperate for love and recognition. Attempting suicide just to find out whether one is loved reflects the poor communication and relationship between that child and the parents or other significant people. Children and adolescents in particular need to see and hear that they are loved. Saying "I love you" and "You are important" is simple, but often is neglected in many families. Love is shown for children and adolescents by the responsibilities, structure, and limits placed on them as they grow. Words are important but are only part of the process.

To Do Something in an Unbearable Situation. This motive suggests that the youth lacks problem-solving skills. Because he or she didn't know how to solve the "problem," the next best thing was to remove himself from it. You can help children and adolescents to solve problems by allowing them the independence to try alternatives. They will experience both failure and success, but they will also build a storehouse of possible solutions to future problems. They can also be taught through examples, modeling, and discussion.

Loss of Control. Suicide is often an impulsive act. Stressors that usually can be handled become overwhelming for any number of reasons. When stress becomes too great, control is lost and behaviors may become erratic. There is confusion of thought; this confusion, along with feelings of being overwhelmed and out of control, impels action, no matter how that action ends. The action is aimed at relieving the stress; when alternatives are limited or blocked, suicide may be the option. This situation is compounded by the use of drugs and/or alcohol, which lower the inhibitions and reduce the fear of death. Once again, parents can help these young people to set priorities and/or to limit their responsibilities and involvements in an effort to control their stress level.

Desire to Die. This motive implies that life is not worth living. There is no hope for the future, and the present offers little. Find out what aspects of life are so terrible to your child that death is the only answer. Show alternative ways of dealing with life's ups and downs. One method is to teach problem-solving skills. Show how change is possible; if necessary and possible, change some of the problems involving you. Discourage isolation and brooding. Encourage more activities in areas where your child will feel some success. Encourage him or her to become involved in activities to help others and to pursue areas of interest or special skills. Physical activity is a great possibility.

Don't be afraid to act on your beliefs and values. Use your authority as a parent in positive, nonaggressive, nonthreatening ways to maintain structure, limits, and control. As long as you use your best judgment in what you think is good and proper for your child, that's all that can be expected.

Many people think that suicide is a way of getting attention, and to some degree it is. In reality, however, it is the act of children and adolescents who feel that life is hopeless. They are often powerless to change or influence the course of their lives or to resolve any specific circumstance. They develop overpowering feelings of hopelessness and helplessness. Because they can see no end to their problems, their solution is suicide.[3]

Appendix

The following are national organizations that can provide general information on suicide.

American Association of Suicidology
2459 South Ash
Denver, CO 80222
(303) 692-0985

The Suicide Research Unit
National Institute of Mental Health
5600 Fishers Lane, Rm. 10C26
Rockville, MD 20857

Youth Suicide National Center
1825 Eye Street N.W., #400
Washington, DC 20006
(202) 429-2016

Suicide Education and Information Center
723 Fourteenth Street N.W., #102
Calgary, Alberta
Canada T2N 2A4
(403) 283-3031

Please check the local services that are available to you and are found in your telephone directory. They will be listed under community mental health centers, hospitals, clinics, psychologists, and psychiatrists.

Notes

Chapter 1

1. D. Shaffer, "Suicide in childhood and early adolescence," *Journal of Child Psychiatry* 15, (1974):275–91.
2. R. E. Gould, "Suicide problems in children and adolescents," *American Journal of Psychotherapy* 19 (1965):228–46.
3. C. Turkington, "Child suicide: An unspoken tragedy," *American Psychological Association Monitor* 14 (1983):15.
4. Center for Disease Control, *Suicide Surveillance Report, Summary: 1970–1980* (U.S. Department of Health and Human Services, Public Health Service, 1985).
5. C. R. Pfeffer, "The distinctive features of children who threaten and attempt suicide," in C. F. Wells and I. R. Stuart (eds.), *Self-Destructive Behavior in Children and Adolescents* (Van Nostrand Reinhold, 1981).
6. N. Lukianowicz, "Attempted suicide in children," *Acta Psychiatrica Scandinavia* 44 (1968):416–34.
7. A. Mattson et al., "Suicidal behavior as a child psychiatric emergency," *Archives of General Psychiatry* 20 (1969):100–109.
8. R. Cohen-Sandler et al., "A follow up study of hospitalized suicidal children," *Journal of the American Academy of Child Psychiatry* 21, 4 (1982):398–403.
9. W. C. Ackerley, "Latency-age children who threaten or attempt to kill themselves," *Journal of the American Academy of Child Psychiatry* 6 (1967):242–61.
10. Cohen-Sandler et al., "A follow up study."
11. Lukianowicz, "Attempted Suicide."
12. C. Pfeffer et al., "Suicidal behavior in latency age children," *Journal of the American Academy of Child Psychiatry* 18 (1979):679–92.
13. I. Orbach et al., "Some common characteristics of latency-age suicidal children: A tentative model based on case study analyses," *Suicide and Life-Threatening Behavior* 11 (1981):3.
14. R. Cohen-Sandler and A. Berman, "Diagnosis and treatment of childhood depression and self-destructive behavior," *Journal of Family Practice* 11 (1980):51–58.
15. L. Ray and N. Johnson, "Adolescent suicide," *Personnel and Guidance Journal*, November 1983, 131–35.
16. J. Hipple and P. Cimbolic, *The Counselor and Suicidal Crisis* (Charles C. Thomas, 1979).

17. Centers for Disease Control, *Suicide Surveillance Report, Summary: 1970–1980* (U.S. Department of Health and Human Services, Public Health Service, 1986).
18. Centers for Disease Control, *Suicide Surveillance Report* (1985).
19. C. Baron, "Child welfare league conference looks at teen suicides in group care," *Network News*, March 1986, 4–5.
20. Shaffer, "Suicide in Childhood."
21. Select Committee on Aging, House of Representatives, *Suicide and Suicide Prevention* (Community Publication No. 98–497, 1985).
22. L. Coleman, "Teen suicide clusters and the Werther effect," *Network News*, March 1986, 1,6,7,8.
23. Ibid.
24. D. P. Phillips, "The influence of suggestion on suicide: Substantive and theoretical implications of the Werther effect," *American Sociological Review* 39, (1979):340–54.
25. D. P. Phillips and L. L. Carstensen, "The clustering of teenage suicides after television news stories about suicide," *New England Journal of Medicine* 315, 11 (1986):685–89.
26. L. Coleman, *Clusters* (Faber and Faber, 1987).
27. E. Shneidman, "At the point of no return," *Psychology Today* 21, 3, March 1987, 54–58.

Chapter 2

1. "The nature and causes of depression—part 1," *Harvard Medical School Mental Health Letter* 4(7):1–4. January 1988.
2. American Psychiatric Association, *Diagnostic and Statistical Manual of Mental Disorders*, 3rd ed. (American Psychiatric Association, 1980).
3. M. Sheperd et al., *Childhood Behavior and Mental Health* (Grune and Stratton, 1971).
4. I. McCaffrey, *Elementary School Children with Persistent Emotional Disturbances* (State Department of Mental Hygiene, New York, 1974).
5. American Psychiatric Association, *Diagnostic and Statistical Manual of Mental Disorders*.

Chapter 3

1. B. Garfinkel and H. Golombek, (1974). "Suicide and depression in childhood and adolescence," *Canadian Medical Association Journal* 110 (1974):1278–81.
2. E. M. Pattison, *The Experience of Dying* (Prentice-Hall, 1977).
3. L. Bender and P. Schilder, "Suicidal preoccupation and attempts in children," *American Journal of Orthopsychiatry* 7 (1937):225–35.
4. J. Jacobs and J. Teicher, "Broken homes and social isolation in at-

tempted suicides of adolescents," *International Journal of Social Psychiatry 13* (1969):139–49.

5. Garfinkel and Golombek, "Suicide and depression in childhood and adolescence."
6. F. Klagsbrun, *Too Young to Die* (Pocket Books, 1981).
7. B. Garfinkel et al., "Suicide attempts in children and adolescents," *American Journal of Psychiatry 139* (1982):10.
8. F. E. Crumley, "The adolescent suicide attempt: A cardinal symptom of a serious psychiatric disorder," *American Journal of Psychotherapy 34* (1982):2.
9. C. R. Pfeffer, "The family system of suicidal children," *American Journal of Psychotherapy 35* (1981):330–41.

Chapter 4

1. M. Shafii et al., "Psychological autopsy of completed suicide in children and adolescents," *American Journal of Psychiatry 142* (1985): 1061–63.

Chapter 5

1. H. Clarizio, "Childhood depression: Diagnosis considerations," *Psychology in the Schools* (1982):181–97.

Chapter 6

1. M. Giffin and C. Felsenthal, *A Cry for Help* (Doubleday, 1983).
2. I. H. Berkovitz, "The role of schools in child, adolescent, and youth suicide prevention," in M. L. Peck, N. L. Farberow, and R. E. Litman (eds.), *Youth Suicide*, (Springer, 1985), 170–90.
3. Ibid.
4. E. S. Stanley and J. T. Barter, "Adolescent suicidal behavior," *American Journal of Orthopsychiatry 40* (1970):87–96.
5. J. D. Teicher and J. Jacobs, "Adolescents who attempt suicide: Preliminary findings," *American Journal of Psychiatry 122* (1966):1248–57.

Chapter 7

1. E. P. Copeland, *Children and Stress* (National Association of School Psychologists, 1989).
2. A. McNamee and J. McNamee, "Stressful life experiences in the early childhood educational setting," in C. R. Wells and I. R. Stuart (eds.), *Self-Destructive Behavior in Children and Adolescents*, (Van Nostrand and Reinhold, 1981).

3. A. Brenner, *Helping Children Cope with Stress* (Lexington Books, 1984).
4. G. E. Vaillant, *Adaptation to Life: How the Best and the Brightest Came of Age* (Little, Brown, 1977).
5. D. Baumrind, "Child care practices anteceding three patterns of pre-school behavior," *Genetic Psychological Monographs* 75 (1967):43–88.
6. M. Haun, *Coping and Defending: Processes of Self-Environment Organization* (Academic Press, 1977).
7. G. F. Melson, "Family adaptation to environmental demands." in H. McCubbin, and C. Figley (eds.), *Stress and the Family, vol. I: Coping with Normative Transitions* (Brunner/Mazel, 1983).
8. Copeland, *Children and Stress.*
9. C. R. Figley and H. I. McCubbin, *Stress and the Family, vol. I: Coping with Normative Transitions* (Brunner/Mazel, 1983).
10. L. H. Frears and J. M. Schneider, "Exploring loss and grief within a holistic framework," *Personnel and Guidance Journal* 22 (1981): 341–45.
11. J. Bowlby, *Attachment and Loss, volume III: Loss: Sadness and Depression* (Basic Books, 1980).
12. C. Jewett, *Helping Children Cope with Separation and Loss* (Harvard Common Press, 1982).
13. Ibid.
14. W. H. Berman and D. C. Turk, "Adaptation to divorce: Problems and coping," *Journal of Marriage and the Family* 43 (1983):11–39.
15. J. Wallerstein and J. Kelly, *Surviving the Breakup: How Children and Parents Cope with Divorce* (Basic Books, 1980).
16. J. J. Neal, "Children's understanding of their parents' divorces," in L. A. Kurdek (ed.), *Children and Divorce* (Jossey-Bass, 1983).
17. Figley and McCubbin, *Stress and the Family.*
18. D. Kandel, "Convergences in prospective longitudinal surveys of drug use in normal populations," in D. Kandel (ed.), *Longitudinal Research in Drug Use: Empirical Findings and Methodological Issues,* (Hemisphere-John Wiley, 1978).
19. M. D. Stanton, "Drugs and the family," *Marriage and Family Review* 2 (1979):1–10.
20. D. F. Duncan, "Family stress and the initiation of adolescent drug abuse: A retrospective study," *Corrective and Social Psychiatry and Journal of Applied Behavior Therapy* 21 (1978):111–14.
21. Figley and McCubbin, *Stress and the Family.*
22. McNamee and McNamee, "Stressful life experiences."
23. L. E. Kopolow, *Handling Stress* (U. S. Government Printing Office, 1987).

Chapter 8

1. M. Peck, "Youth suicide," *Death Education* 6 (1982):29–47.
2. B. Garfinkel et al., "Suicide attempts in children and adolescents," *American Journal of Psychiatry,* 139 (1982):10.

3. C. R. Pfeffer, "The distinctive features of children who threaten and attempt suicide." In C. F. Wells and I. R. Stuart (eds.), *Self-Destructive Behavior in Children and Adolescents* (New York: Van Nostrand Reinhold, 1981).
4. K. McCoy, *Coping with Teenage Depression: A Parent's Guide* (New American Library, 1982).
5. M. Lieberman and M. Hardie, *Resolving Family and Other Conflicts* (Cymbidium Books, 1981).
6. "Father of teen suicide victim sues school officials," *New Haven Register*, 6 (January 1987):1–2.
7. T. Gordon, *Parent Effectiveness Training* (New American Library, 1975).
8. Ibid.
9. T. Good and J. Brophy, *Looking in Classrooms* (Harper and Row, 1978).

Chapter 9

1. T. Gordon, *Parent Effectiveness Training* (New American Library, 1975).
2. D. Dinkmeyer and G. D. McKay, *Parent's Handbook: Systematic Training for Effective Parenting* (American Guidance Service, 1982).
3. M. L. Silberman and S. A. Wheelan, *How to Discipline without Feeling Guilty* (Research Press, 1980).
4. Dinkmeyer and McKay, *Parent's Handbook*.
5. S. Lerman, *Parent Awareness: Positive Parenting for the 1980s* (Winston Press, 1980).
6. Silverman and Wheelan, *How to Discipline*.
7. Ibid.
8. Ibid.
9. Ibid.
10. M. Lieberman and M. Hardie, *Resolving Family and Other Conflicts* (Cymbidium Books, 1981).
11. A. Mehrabian, *Nonverbal Communication* (Aldine-Atherton, 1972).

Chapter 10

1. N. H. Allen and M. Peck, *Suicide in Young People* (American Association of Suicidology, 1977).
2. K. A. Slaikeu, *Crisis Intervention: A Handbook for Practice and Research* (Allyn and Bacon, 1984).

Chapter 11

1. E. A. Taylor and S. A. Stansfield, "Children Who Poison Themselves: I. Clinical Comparison with Psychiatric Controls" and "II. Prediction of

Attendance for Treatment," *British Journal of Psychiatry* 145 (1984):127–35.

2. K. Hawton and J. Catalan, *Attempted Suicide: A Practical Guide to Its Nature and Management* (University Press, 1987).

3. P. G. Patros and T. K. Shamoo. *Depression and Suicide in Children and Adolescents* (Allyn and Bacon, 1989).

Index

About the Authors

TONIA K. SHAMOO, Ph.D., is co-author with Philip G. Patros of *Depression and Suicide in Children and Adolescents*. She is a licensed psychologist and has a private practice in psychotherapy. She is also a consultant to various school systems and conducts workshops and seminars on the topics of depression and suicide. Dr. Shamoo has been awarded the Distinguished Service Award by the Connecticut Association of School Psychologists for her dedication and commitment to the well-being of children and adolescents.

PHILIP G. PATROS, Ph.D., is a licensed psychologist and a professor in the Department of Counseling and School Psychology at Southern Connecticut State University. He maintains a private practice in psychological services and conducts workshops and seminars dealing with depression and suicide in children and adolescents. He is co-author with Tonia K. Shamoo of *Depression and Suicide in Children and Adolescents*. Dr. Patros has had a long and distinguished career working with children and adolescents and has been awarded the Distinguished Service Award by the Connecticut Association of School Psychologists.